Hegel's Philosophy of Right, with Marx's Commentary:

a Handbook for Students

Hegel's Philosophy of Right, with Marx's Commentary:
a Handbook for Students

by

HOWARD P. KAINZ

MARTINUS NIJHOFF/THE HAGUE/1974

PRINTED IN THE NETHERLANDS

TABLE OF CONTENTS

GENERAL INTRODUCTION

The Place of Hegel in the History of Philosophy   1
The Importance of Hegel's Philosophy   2
The Importance of Hegel's "Philosophy of Right"   4
Hegel's "System"   5
The Dialectic   6
Hegel's Terminology   9
    Marx's Critique of the Philosophy of Right   11
    Sample Examination Questions & Term Paper Topics   12

ANALYSIS OF HEGEL'S "PHILOSOPHY OF RIGHT"

THE PREFACE TO THE 'PHILOSOPHY OF RIGHT'   13

THE INTRODUCTION TO THE P.R. (§§ 1–33)   14
    Sample exam questions, sample essays   16

    Diagram of the development of the *Philosophy of Right*   17

I. ABSTRACT RIGHT (§§ 4–104)   18
    Sample exam questions, sample essay   21

II. MORALITY (§§ 105–141)   22
    Sample exam questions, term paper topic   24

III. ETHICAL LIFE (§§ 142–360)   25
    Term paper topic   26

    1. The Family (§§ 158–181)   27
        A. The stage of love and marriage   27
        B. Family capital   29
        C. Education of children and dissolution of the family   29
           Sample exam questions, etc.   31

2. Civil Society (§§ 182–256)   32
    A. The system of needs   33
       1) The development of need and satisfaction into "genera"   33
       2) The development of work into "genera"   34
       3) Resources   34
          a) The agricultural class   35
          b) The business class   35
          c) The bureaucracy   35
    B. The administration of justice   36
       1) The process by which right becomes law   36
       2) The process by which law becomes existent   37
       3) The process by which existent law vindicates itself through judge-
          ments   38
          a) The process of inquiry   38
          b) The stages of legal action   39
          c) The process of legal judgement   39
    C. The police and the corporation   40
       1) The police   40
       2) The corporation   41
       Sample exam questions, etc.   42

3. The State (§§ 257–360)   44
    A. The constitution   44
       Marx's commentary   47
       1) The inner constitution of the state, in its existence-for-self   50
          Marx's commentary   51
       a) The crown   52
          Marx's commentary   54
       b) The executive   60
          Marx's commentary   61
       c) The legislature   64
          Marx's commentary   66
       2) Sovereignty in relation to foreign states   76
    B. International law   77
    C. World history   78
       Sample exam questions, etc.   79
       Appendix, Marx's commentary   82
       Selected bibliography   84

Index of Names   85

Subject Index   86

GENERAL INTRODUCTION
GEORG WILHELM FRIEDRICH HEGEL (1770–1831)

THE PLACE OF HEGEL IN THE HISTORY OF PHILOSOPHY

In order to gain a proper perspective of Hegel's place in the history of philosophy, it might be useful to focus on one key concept which has evolved significantly in meaning, from the time of Aristotle to Hegel. I am speaking of the philosophical concept of the "category."

In Aristotle's system, there were ten categories (or "predicaments") of reality or being. These included substantiality, time, place, quantity, quality, and other aspects of knowable beings. The most notable thing about these categories is that they all have to do with what we would call "objective" realities. That is, none of them purport to describe subjective or mental states or conditions.

In modern philosophy (i.e., philosophy since the time of Descartes), there was a swing of the pendulum in the opposite direction, from objectivity to subjectivity – culminating in the twelve *new* "categories" of Kant. All of Kant's categories were subjective ways of looking at reality: We can organize objective phenomena into universal unities; therefore the first Kantian category is "unity." We can separate objective phenomena into particular divisions; therefore the second category is "plurality." And so forth.

With Hegel, the modern trend to subjectivism is arrested, and we have, not surprisingly, a new type of "category" – the category of the unity of thought and being, of self and other, of *subject and object*. Hegel reacted to what he called the extreme "subjectivism" of Kant. And it was his intention to restore objectivity to its proper place in philosophy; without, however, regressing to the objectivism of Aristotle. Therefore the vantage point which he chooses is an attempted compromise between empiricism (emphasis on objective facts and events) and idealism (emphasis on subjective categories and ideas). And his primary concern, in most of his writings, is to capture the "movement," or oscillation, that takes place between the two poles of objectivity and subjectivity. For example, in his *Philosophy of Right*, he is

primarily interested in showing the *relationship between* the subjective freedom of the individual and the objective political, legal and social structures
to be found in society.

It is sometimes suggested that Hegel initiated a complete breakthrough in
philosophy, coming up with a completely new "system." However, the originality of Hegel is easily exaggerated. His method of "triplicity" (the dialectical "movement" from existence-in-self to existence-for-self to existence
in-and-for-self) was inspired by Kant (as Hegel himself avers in his *History
of Philosophy* and other places). "Phenomenology," in Hegel's estimation,
also began with Kant, and not with Hegel's *Phenomenology of Mind*. The
"Absolute Self-Consciousness" which Hegel refers to in various writings is
simply a further extension of Kant's "transcendental unity of apperception."
The Hegelian "category" of thought/being was inspired by the ego/non-ego
of Fichte and the subject-object of Schelling. Fichte and Schelling, contem-
poraries of Hegel, were likewise responsible for early attempts at writing a
phenomenological history of the development of human consciousness –
attempts that Hegel brings to a final conclusion with his famous *Phenomenology*.

Finally, we might note that Hegel's attempt to synthesize all of reality
into a complete system of knowledge was perhaps the least original idea of
all. Aristotle and Spinoza had both attempted to do this. Fichte, also engaged
in system-building – although his efforts were less persevering and complete
than Hegel's.

This is not to say that Hegel was not original, but only to reiterate one of
Hegel's own observations: that every man is the product of his age. What we
refer to as "originality" very often consists in simply giving a new direction
to currents that have already been set in motion.

THE IMPORTANCE OF HEGEL'S PHILOSOPHY

Even if the philosophy of Hegel were of no particular importance in itself, it
would still have an historical importance in view of philosophical movements
that it has given rise to. There are three philosophical movements that are
closely related to Hegelianism: existentialism, phenomenology, and Marxism.

Existentialism: Kierkegaard, sometimes called the "father" of existentialism, hardly ever refers to Hegel except to criticize him. However, many of the
prime "existential" concepts expounded by Kierkegaard bear unmistakable
traces of Hegelian influence. For example, Kierkegaard's thesis that quantitative progressions can lead eventually to a qualitative "leap" is found in a

different context in the Preface to Hegel's *Phenomenology*; his contention that historical "proofs" for Christianity are invalid was first expounded by Hegel; his exposition of the "task" bears strong resemblances to Hegel's exposition of "work" in the *Phenomenology;* and his "Knight of Faith" is apparently a reformulation of Hegel's "Knight of Virtue." Many other instances could be cited to show that Hegel supplied the main impetus or springboard for some of the key concepts of Kierkegaard's existentialism.

Phenomenology: It is very hard to find any hard and fast definition of "phenomenology" from contemporary phenomenologists. Hegel seems to be one of the first persons to use this term to describe a particular approach in philosophy. He defines "phenomenology" as a philosophical position which concentrates on the distinction between subject and object, and tries to discover which aspects of reality are derived from the subject (or ego), and which aspects are primarily attributable to the object (or thing-in-itself). He states that Kant, who was primarily concerned with showing how many supposedly "objective" realities are caused by subjective presuppositions, was a "phenomenologist."

Contemporary phenomenology stems from Husserl who, like Kant, was concerned with isolating the "a priori" subjective constructs which enter into our "objective" knowledge. For this reason, Husserl would also seem to be a "phenomenologist" in the original Hegelian sense of that word.

Marxism: Marx in his early years was a member of the "Young Hegelian" movement, and retained a respect and admiration for Hegel throughout his career. In fact, as an old man he confided to a friend that he had always wanted to write a book explaining the philosophy of Hegel to the common man in simple language.

Marx, however, like Kierkegaard, presents Hegel in a very much altered form. According to Marx, a distinction has to be made between the Hegelian *system* and Hegel's dialectical *method*. The system is introverted and rationalistic, putting imaginary "spiritual" values before practical and material values. The system has to be "overturned," so that reality (material and practical values) will once again take precedence over "fantasy." The Hegelian method, however, should be retained. By utilizing Hegel's dialectical method in scientific fashion we can reliably predict and control changes which take place in the socio-economic sphere (the sphere of primary interest to Marx).

We shall examine Hegel's dialectic method in more detail in a section which follows, entitled "Dialectic."

THE IMPORTANCE OF HEGEL'S "PHILOSOPHY OF RIGHT"

First of all, it should be mentioned that the title of this book *The Philosophy of Right*, can be somewhat misleading. From the title, we might surmise that the book has to do with various human rights, such as the right to life and property, and perhaps also with law, insofar as law is oriented to defining and protecting the rights of individuals. Our suspicion would be correct to a certain extent. Hegel's *Philosophy of Right* does have to do with such things. But it is also a treatise on political philosophy and a textbook on moral philosophy. In Hegel's estimation, "right" and "law" (although differing from morality) are inseparably connected with morality; and morality is inseparably connected with social and political structures. And the *Philosophy of Right* attempts to show these interconnections in a systematic fashion, proceeding a) from right and law, to b) morality, to c) political philosophy.

The third and final section, on political philosophy, seems to have been the most influential, giving impetus to such diverse movements as communism and national socialism (Naziism), and even (according to Bosanquet) supplying new theoretical bases for democracy:

Communism: During the 1840's, when Marx made the transition from "Leftist" Hegelianism to communism, he wrote a treatise entitled *A Critique of Hegel's "Philosophy of Right,"* which has only recently been subjected to close study by scholars. In this Critique, we find that Marx, by applying a "transformative criticism" to Hegel, has already formulated some of the pivotal concepts that will receive expression later on (in the *Communist Manifesto, Capital,* and other more mature works) – such as the concept of a "proletariat," and the necessity for abolition of private property and the State. An analysis of this Critique is given in this handbook at the end of the various sections on which Marx commented.

National Socialism: As Peter Viereck points out in his book on the development of Naziism (*Metapolitics;* Capricorn, 1965), Hegel supplied some of the pivotal concepts which gave rise to the National Socialist movement in Hitler's Germany. For example, Hegel stressed the "organic" nature of the State, and the Nazis extrapolated this idea to preach that the German nation was an organism which had to follow its own laws of growth, without being hindered by conventional moral standards. Likewise, the Nazis misinterpreted Hegel's famous statement, "The Rational is the Real," as meaning that a nation's policies are correct ("rational") when they are successful (realistic, or "real").

Democracy: According to Bosanquet, Hegel's *Philosophy of Right* is very important insofar as it brings out in the open one of the "paradoxes" of democracy – the fact that maximum individual freedom can only be found in a complex and highly organized political structure. In Hegel's political philosophy we get beyond the "myth" of democracy – the illusion that the state is just a superstructure created by millions of individuals who choose, through a "social contract," to sacrifice part of their individual freedom to achieve common objectives. According to Hegel's analysis, both individuality and freedom are to a great extent *results* of a complex cultural milieu, including the modern "State." A person who is brought up in a primitive society, or without the benefit of multiple social interactions, will encounter almost insuperable obstacles in becoming an individual, or in achieving the sense of right and responsibility that goes hand in hand with "freedom."

HEGEL'S "SYSTEM"

In the prime of his life, Hegel wrote his famous "system" of philosophy, which was entitled *The Encyclopedia of Philosophy*. This Encyclopedia consisted of 3 major sections, 1) the *Logic*, 2) the *Philosophy of Nature*, and 3) the *Philosophy of Spirit*. The *Philosophy of Right* fits into the third section, as may be seen from the following brief summary of the *Encyclopedia:*

The Encyclopedia of Philosophy

I. Logic
There is a gradual transition from simple *ideas* of quantity, quality, etc., to *ideas* of scientific *laws* (cause and effect, action and reaction, substance and accident), to the *laws governing ideas* (i. e., logic in the usual sense – the study of judgments, syllogisms). Finally, we advance from the consideration of the laws of ideas to a consideration of the varieties of *being* (which correspond to our ideas). And this brings us to...

II. The Philosophy of Nature
We begin with "mere" being – matter, motion, space and time – and make a gradual transition to those types of being which are closest to *consciousness* – plants and animals. This final contact with consciousness then leads us on to the next major stage, which is....

III. The Philosophy of Spirit

We start with "mere" consciousness – the soul of a human being, or "subjective spirit," as Hegel calls it. In order to complete our examination of subjective spirit, we find it necessary to take into account the objective legal, moral, social and political structures in which the individual "soul" exists. These objective structures are what Hegel calls "Objective Spirit," or "Spirit Objectified." The philosophical analysis of these structures is called the Philosophy of Right.

Finally, it is necessary to examine the means by which these objective structures affect, and are affected by, individual consciousnesses. According to Hegel, the means by which this mutual interaction takes place are art, religion, and philosophy; and it is to these three topics that he devotes the last sections of the *Encyclopedia* (entitled "Absolute Spirit").

As may be seen from the above summary, the *Encyclopedia of Philosophy* is certainly not an encyclopedia in the usual sense of that word. The topics are not arranged in any alphabetical order, but seem to lead into each other. Earlier topics lead into later topics through Hegel's dialectical logic, which is a "logic of movement." We shall discuss this dialectical logic in the next section.

It should be noted that the "Philosophy of Right," in the context of the *Encyclopedia*, is simply a segment of the *Philosophy of Spirit*. However Hegel, towards the end of his career, expanded this segment into a book. And so, when we speak of Hegel's *Philosophy of Right*, we are referring not to the segment of the Encyclopedia on that subject, but to the book which was written as an expansion of that segment.

THE DIALECTIC

It might be best to begin our discussion of Hegel's "dialectical" logic with a couple of examples to illustrate the basic principle of dialectic:

First of all, consider the example of a *dialogue*: When you are engaging in a dialogue with another person, you ordinarily start with certain opinions or presuppositions. The other person opposes you, and offers counterbalancing points of view. Then finally, after some constructive dialogue, you may come to an agreement on certain points, resulting in a new formulation – a *compromise* statement that you both can agree to. Let us call your original opinions or presuppositions the "thesis"; the opposing viewpoints of the other person the "antithesis"; and the compromise agreement the "synthesis."*

As a second example, consider the functions of moral ideals in your own practical activity: You begin with a "thesis," a certain moral aspiration that you would like to put into effect. But you encounter difficulties, or antitheses: either you do not have the physical or psychological strength to accomplish these moral goals, or certain conditions in your environment prevent you from attaining them. You then have a choice of either abandoning these goals in futile desperation, or revising them so as to make them more realistic and attainable. If you choose the second alternative, you have arrived at a "synthesis," in the context of your own personal aspirations.

Generalizing from these two examples, we see that the "thesis" is some starting point in life; the "antithesis" is some obstacle in life which threatens the validity of the thesis in the form in which it is presented; the "synthesis," finally, is a reformulation of the thesis in such a way as to allow it to survive its encounter with the antithesis, without being lost or destroyed.

This constant transition from thesis to antithesis to synthesis is called "dialectical logic," or the logic of contradiction. It is a major element in all the writings of Hegel.** However, depending on the context, it may be applied by Hegel from three different "points of view":

1) When Hegel is speaking of an external object, or "being...
The thesis (A) is a situation in which one aspect (x) of the object is explicit to the observer, while another aspect (y) is still implicit or hidden. As the observer analyzes the object in depth, he discovers the aspect y, which temporarily becomes all-important, and excludes x from consideration (so that y becomes the antithesis (B) to x.) Finally, after mature reflection, the observer comes to see the relation of his new discovery (y) to his old knowledge (x) about the object .And the final realization of the way in which the object manifests both these aspects (xy) is the resulting synthesis (C).

* Hegel himself rarely uses the terms "thesis-antithesis-synthesis." But these terms are very often usefully employed in explaining the Hegelian dialectic, as an approximation to the more precise Hegelian terms, "existence-in-self," "existence-for-self," and "existence-in-and-for-self." ("Existence" here means be-ing, i.e. the act of being.)

** For a more extensive discussion of dialectic than is feasible here, see my *Hegel's "Phenomenology," Part I: Analysis and Commentary* (University of Alabama Press, 1974), Ch. VI.

2) When Hegel is speaking of consciousness, or the ego...

The thesis (A) is a state of consciousness in which a certain idea or opinion (x) is held explicitly by the ego, while an apparently contradictory idea or opinion is suppressed. As an individual matures in his reflections, the opinion y seems to be worthy of more serious consideration than he had previously attached to it. Then y becomes predominant, and takes the place of x (in the antithesis (B)). But finally the individual comes to see that, in a certain sense, y is not necessarily incompatible with x, and he manages to reconcile his new insight (y) with his former vantage point (x), thus attaining to a synthesis (xy) in the third moment (C).

3) When Hegel is considering "Spirit"... *

The thesis (A) is a situation in which a subject, or an ego (x) encounters an object, an objective law, an objective idea, an objective event, or an objective person – any of which might be designated as "y". In the antithesis (B), y eludes the grasp of x, by demonstrating certain properties or potentialities that x had not been previously aware of. In the synthesis (C), after y has demonstrated its independence, a new existential union takes place between x and y, a union which leaves room for, and gives recognition to, the independence and distinction of y from x.

If we would apply this analysis of dialectical logic in a very general way to Hegel's *Philosophy of Right*, we would have to say first of all that the *Philosophy of Right* is written from the *third* point of view, the point of view of "Spirit." The "thesis" is presented in the introductory chapters, in which Hegel analyzes the "immediate" encounter of a free individual with private property, laws, right and wrong. The "antithesis" is presented in the chapter on "morality" in which property rights, human rights, and laws seem to take on the aspect of universal, objective norms ("oughts") which are beyond the grasp of men, but to which men must submit. Finally, in the third and longest section (the "synthesis"), there is an examination of the family, "civil society," and the state, in which there is a gradual reconciliation of freedom and necessity, of subjective needs and objective norms.

There are other minor triads in the *Philosophy of Right*. For example, within the "thesis" there is a triad of indeterminate will (a thesis), determinate will (an antithesis), and absolute will (a synthesis). There is another minor triad of thesis-antithesis-synthesis *within* the major antithesis (morality).

* "Spirit" is a technical term often used by Hegel to denote the union and reciprocity *between* subjectivity and objectivity.

And so forth. But it is not necessary to go into all these minor triads at this point, since our purpose here is just to introduce the general triadic structure of dialectical logic.

HEGEL'S TERMINOLOGY

There are some technical terms used by Hegel which have meanings which differ from ordinary parlance. It is important to discuss some of these terms before proceeding into a detailed analysis of Hegel's *Philosophy of Right:*

"*Existence-in-self*"* *(ansichsein)* corresponds, in general, to the "thesis" (see the preceding section on "Dialectical Logic"). In the Introduction to the *Philosophy of Right*, we begin with free will as an "in-itself," because the will in the beginning (before choices are made) is indeterminate; that is, it has not yet been expressed or determined.

"*Existence-for-self*"* *(fürsichsein)* corresponds to the "antithetical" moment. In the Introduction to the *Philosophy of Right* (to return to the example we used above) the will overcomes its indetermination, makes choices, and thus expresses itself in various ways. It passes from potential decision-making to actual decision-making. In Hegel's terminology the will comes to exist "for-itself."

"*Existence-in-and-for-self*" *(an-und-fürischsein)* corresponds to the moment of "synthesis." In the Introduction to the *Philosophy of Right*, the will finally comes to the point where it unites the non-self-determination of "existence-in-self" with the self-determination of "existence for-self." How? By a subtle paradox: It *determines* itself to *be* determined by society, by culture, by the state. It consciously, *voluntarily* immerses itself in its social and political milieu, to be shaped and directed by that milieu. Thus, in a certain sense, it is *not* self-determined (since it is being determined by society); but in another sense, it *is* self-determined (since it has voluntarily *chosen* to be determined by society).

Existence-in-and-for-self will very often result in such paradoxical situations in the writings of Hegel.

The "particular": The particular is a part which only has meaning in the context of some whole. For example, an isolated human being is particular, in relation to the society of which he is a part.

* Jean Paul Sartre uses the terms "in-itself" (*en soi*) and "for-itself" (*pour soi*) in a sense which is partly the same as, partly different from, Hegel's usage. If the student is familiar with the Sartrean connotation of these terms, it would be better to forget these connotations for the present, since Sartre uses the terms in a limited and derived sense, as compared with Hegel.

The "universal": The universal can have two significations in Hegel: In its first signification, it is the whole which gives meaning to component parts; for example, society gives meaning to its component persons. In its second signification, universality is the dialectical interaction or reciprocity between the whole and its parts; for example, we could say that the essential thing in political philosophy is neither particular persons, nor society, but the relation between these particular persons and their society – the active contribution which these persons make to their society, and the channels which are set up by a society to determine the needs of the people which it serves and represents.

The "individual" is a particular which actively and manifestly affirms its relationship to the universal. For example, a particular person is truly an "individual" when he actively demonstrates that he embodies the cultural traits of his society in some unique way.

"Abstract" in Hegel is an adjective which signifies "isolation from context.' For example, a sense impression, isolated from its spatial or temporal context would be abstract. Likewise a particular human being (e.g., a hermit) who withdrew from his social context would be living an "abstract" existence.

"Concrete" is an adjective which signifies "united with its context." For example, what *we* call an "abstract idea" would be called "concrete" by *Hegel*, if it is considered in the context of the appropriate ideas or sense impressions which gave rise to it. Likewise, a political State is "concrete" when it is in active and constant rapport with the citizens composing it.

"Science" for Hegel is preeminently his dialectical philosophy. "Speculation" and "Reason" are synonyms for Science in this sense.

The "Absolute" is a complete union of objectivity (in some sense) with subjectivity (in some sense). For example, "Absolute Knowledge" at the end of Hegel's *Phenomenology* is the final union of Consciousness with Self-Consciousness; the "Absolute Idea" at the end of Hegel's *Logic* is the complete unity of Being with Thought; and "Absolute Will" in Hegel's *Philosophy of Right* is the complete union of the subjective power of free choice with the objective content of freedom.

"Spirit" or "Mind" is the translation often given for Hegel's term, *Geist*. It does *not* mean a subjective quality or faculty. Rather, it signifies the union of consciousness and "Nature."

"Understanding" is the human faculty which is primary in ordinary formal logic and in the physical sciences.

"Reason" is the faculty which goes beyond Understanding to use "dialectical" logic and to create Speculative Ideas (i.e., true Science, in Hegel's

sense of that word). It is the power to comprehend the unity of opposites.

The "*Idea*" is a "concrete" unity of subjective insight and objective reality. There is only *one* Idea; but this one Idea has numerous manifestations or explications (e.g., the various manifestations of the Idea in Hegel's *Logic*).

The "*Concept*" ordinarily means an intermediate stage of the Idea. There is only one Concept, which explicates itself in various ways, producing what we call "concepts."

"*Immediate*" as an adjective means "pristine," "undeveloped." For example, the family is an "immediate" ethical structure, because it is a natural prerequisite for "civil society"; "civil society," on the other hand, is an elaboration of basic familial existence, and thus a "*mediated*" stage.

MARX'S CRITIQUE OF HEGEL'S "PHILOSOPHY OF RIGHT"

Marx was about twenty-five years of age when he wrote a commentary on §§ 261–311 of Hegel's *Philosophy of Right*, which dealt with the "constitution" of the state in accord with the triadic division of the constitution into a) the Crown; b) the Executive; and c) the Legislative.

This commentary of Marx was written at a time when Marx was just making the transition from the Young Hegelian movement to communism. In the commentary, Marx uses "transformative criticism" to de-mystify Hegel, and comes up with some seminal ideas which will be of pivotal importance in his later works – for example, the notion that the proletariat, and not the bureocracy, constitute the "universal class"; the notion that private property and primogeniture give rise to alienation; and the suggestion that future social progress will require the abolition of "the state" as an institution determining man's destiny.

Although this commentary does not have the polish and lucidity of Marx's mature works, it is important insofar as it gives us a chart of Marx's own intellectual path to the ideas of the *Communist Manifesto* – a path which at that time was primarily philosophical since Marx had not yet begun his extensive and scholarly research in the works of Adam Smith, Ricardo, Say, and other economists.

In commenting on Hegel, Marx ordinarily quotes a section from Hegel and follows up with his comments and criticisms. In our analysis, (which in this handbook is appended to each of the relevant sub-sections of part III, 3A, 1) we will concentrate on some of the major passages from Hegel on which Marx focuses, and provide a summary of Marx's observations with respect to that passage. Where page numbers are given, these are all references to the

O'Malley-Jolin edition of Marx's *Critique of Hegel's Philosophy of Right* (Cambridge, 1971). Paragraph numbers are references to the Knox translation of Hegel's *Philosophy of Right*.

SAMPLE EXAMINATION QUESTIONS

1. What is meant by Hegel's "dialectical method"? Explain how the dialectical method applies to "things," or beings.
2. Show how law, morality and political philosophy are interrelated in Hegel's *Philosophy of Objective Spirit*.
3. In what sense did Hegel's philosophy lead to Marxism?
4. Contrast the usual meaning of the following terms with Hegel's special meaning: "Science"; "Mind"; "Idea"; "concrete"; "Reason."

TERM PAPER TOPICS

1. *Hegel's use of the terms "concrete," "abstract," "moment," and "alienation."* Consult George Kline's article, "Some Recent Reinterpretations of Hegel's Philosophy," in *The Monist*, Vol. 48, No. 1, Jan., 1964.

2. *The influence of Hegel upon Kierkegaard and Marx.* See Karl Löwith's *From Hegel to Nietzsche* (Doubleday Anchor) for an account of Kierkegaard's theistic and Marx's atheistic response to Hegel.

3. *The general structure of Hegel's Philosophy of Right.* K.-H. Ilting has an essay on "The Structure of Hegel's *Philosophy of Right*" in *Hegel's Political Philosophy*, Z.A. Pelczynski ed., (see Bibliography).

Hegel. *The Philosophy of Right*, T. M. Knox tr. (London: Oxford University Press, 1967)

HEGEL'S PREFACE*

Political philosophers these days are bringing disrepute on the science of Philosophy. They spend their time trying to find a basis for the state in "nature"; or weaving webs of mystical intuition and feeling; or straining to keep philosophy "in vogue," by overthrowing all of its rational principles. The characteristic that all these philosophers have in common is their distrust of, and opposition to *reason* – and by "reason" I mean the synthesis of universality and particularity. They seem never to have realized that perhaps they might profitably turn their attention to the way in which universal and particular are synthesized in an actual *state*, and on this basis formulate the *manifestations* of reason in the explicit systematic *form* of reason (rather than merely applying the dead categories of traditional logic in an arbitrary way to arbitrary content, after the manner of our predecessors).

When I recommend concentration upon the actual state, I am not implying that philosophy should resign itself to the *status quo* (and hope for some better world in the afterlife). But the subjectivists and intuitionists make themselves ridiculous in the attitude they take towards the realities of life. What good does it do to pine after some ideal order, which has no roots in the existent rational order? What good does it do to spend one's life analyzing the "ought" in the practical sphere, to the extent of deciding (like Plato) how nurses are to take care of the young, or to the extent of deciding (like Fichte) whether passports should include pictures as well as signatures?

Yes, we should recognize an ought, but only that ought which "is." The business of political philosophy is to elaborate the basic rational structures in society, to show the wedding of thought and fact, the union of form and content, the merger of the "is" *and* the "ought." The rational comprehension of this union *is* what *ought* to be – and this is the fulfillment of the existence of a society.

* In order to avoid the frequent use of "Hegel says," "Hegel thinks," etc., I have simply paraphrased Hegel's ideas in the following sections. Any additional comments added *to* Hegel's ideas, will be given in footnotes.

But this fulfillment must wait for the proper moment. For it is only when a state arrives at the grey dusk of its maturity, that philosophy can paint its "grey on grey," comprehending what has happened; without, however, being able to change everything back again into a vernal green.

HEGEL'S INTRODUCTION

The subject-matter of the philosophy of right is the *concept** of right. The concept of right results from the various ways in which the will enters into interaction with the external world. This interaction results in the emergence of civil rights and property rights, of law and morality, and of institutions such as the family and the state. The totality of all these results may be called the "system of right."

The system of right is rather paradoxical. On the one hand, it appears as something objectively existent. For example, we think of civil laws as being objective norms to which we all must adhere. But a little reflection leads us to the realization that all such laws must have been created during some particular space of time by some particular individual (or individuals). And we could say the same thing about property rights, moral laws, and social institutions.

It is the purpose of this book to examine the system of right in the light of this paradox. Thus, for example, when we consider *law* , we are not concerned with "positive" law, which is primarily an objective concatenation of the laws prevailing in some society. Rather, it is more in line with our philosophical goals to examine "natural" law, i.e., the emergence of rational, *objectively* valid laws from the will of particular subjectivities. This is a phenomenon which is not touched upon by the experts in positive law, and is more particularly a topic for philosophical investigation.

Let us begin, then, with an analysis of the will. After this we will proceed to discuss the various ways in which the will is related to the various "objective" aspects of the system of right.

The movement or operation of the will can be divided up into three distinct "moments."**:

* "Concept" is used here in the technical Hegelian sense. It does not mean an "abstract idea," but an actual state of union *between* the world and consiousness. Hegel believes that it is possible to describe *this* state of union in the same way that it is possible to describe some state of affairs *within* the external world or *within* consciousness.

** These moments do not follow one another in temporal succession. They are simultaneous. But at any given time, one moment may be emphasized over another; or we, in our analysis, may give consideration to one moment in preference to others. This causes the "emergence" of a distinct moment.

1) The moment of indetermination: This is the moment of negation, in which an individual will "withdraws" psychically from concrete circumstances, from natural necessities, from its own desires, and even from its own ideas. This psychic withdrawal ultimately will result in the creation of what we call the "person" (considered as an abstract unit of individuality). When it is carried to extremes, it results in political anarchy, masochistic asceticism, and religious nihilism – i.e., individualism of an extremely negativistic kind.

2) The moment of determination: This is the negation of the previous negation. And since a double negation results in an affirmation, this moment results in a positive relationship to one's external environment, to one's needs and desires, and to one's own ideas. Through the volitional processes of decision-making, consent, action, and creativity, the will gives determination not only to the external world but also to itself.

3) Absolute will results from the realization a) that the "indeterminate" will is really determinate, insofar as it creates a determinate person; b) that the "determinate" will is really indeterminate, insofar as the act of determination involves the application of the universal (the indeterminate) to the particular; and c) that what we call the "will" is nothing but the constant oscillation between these two moments.

The absolute will, therefore, is not concerned merely a) with the act of negation and withdrawal, as a means of affirming personal individuality; nor b) with the process of decision-making, by which an individual chooses between various types of content; but c) with maintaining a constant rapport between the individual and "the universal." But the "universality" to which the individual becomes related passes through three successive stages*: First, it is the right-to-property, through which personalities gradually express themselves and mutually define their limits: Then it takes the form of an abstract ideal – the moral law, as the objective norm by which men strive to regulate their actions. Finally, "universality" comes to imply concrete social relationships – the family, civil society, and the state.

It should be emphasized that all these various relationships to universality are *reciprocal* relationships: The individual is changed and measured by them and they in turn are conditioned and indeed created by individuals.

---

* These "three stages" are discussed in Hegel's *Philosophy of Mind*, pp. 487ff., as well as the *Philosophy of Right*, p. 33ff.

SAMPLE EXAMINATION QUESTIONS

1. Hegel rejects utopian ideas of a perfect state, as unrealistic "oughts." What does he propose as a substitute for such "oughts"?
2. What is the technical Hegelian meaning of "Concept"? (see Glossary, p. 12) How is the "concept of right" a manifestation of this general technical meaning?

SAMPLE ESSAYS

Sometimes people define freedom as "not being determined by external circumstances." Sometimes they speak of it as the "right of self-determination." The first meaning is similar to what Hegel calls the "indeterminate will"; the second reminds us of the "determinate will." Analyze these and other popular conceptions of freedom, in terms of Hegel's triadic division of the "moments" of the will. The "absolute will" is a peculiarly Hegelian conception of freedom, insofar as it is a union of opposites. Are there any parallels to the "absolute will" in popular modern conceptions of freedom?

SCHEMATIC DIAGRAM OF THE STRUCTURE OF THE PHILOSOPHY OF RIGHT

(downward arrows show simple transitions or movements; upward arrows show major, "pivotal" transitions which give rise to more advanced stages).

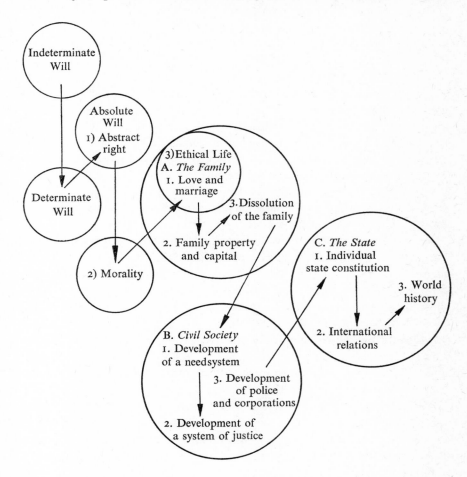

Part. I. ABSTRACT RIGHT

The will, in its phase of "indeterminacy" (see p. 15 above) withdraws psychically from its surroundings. Let us take a further look at these "surroundings": They include particular objects, places, and events; particular people; particular feelings, ideas and sense impressions; and even one's own body, insofar as it becomes manifest as a particular object in the world. In short, by an act of psychic "negation" we are able to "remove" ourselves from involvement with all particular, finite things. But if the will can negate all finite things, how can it itself be finite? It must in some sense be outside the finite. And if it is outside the finite, it must be "infinite."

When we think of the will as "infinite," and as standing in contrast to all that is finite, we have arrived at the concept of an individual who is not immersed in the world of particularity, but is in some sense able to escape from it by an act of the will. This "escape" may take the form of abstract withdrawal or fanaticism, as sometimes happens in the phase of "indeterminacy." Now (in the "absolute" phase of will) it may connote a simple relationship of self-identity and self-consciousness – the realization that at one and the same time I (a) am this particular individual, but (b) because of my power of thought and will I am not *restricted* to my bodily personality. This latter realization is the idea of a free *personality*.

Therefore, when I think of myself as a "person," I have a vague intimation that I am a center, an infinite self-relation, existing outside the borders of everything that is determinate and finite,* and yet at the same time in intimate contact and reciprocity with the determinate and finite.

Some philosophers, who understand personality as a static indeterminacy and an abstract self-identity, believe that the idea of *human equality* is derived from personality. Every person, according to them, is an abstract unit

---

* This is the source for such notions as the existence of a "beyond" or a heaven, and the notion of the possibility of personal immortality. Hegel shows how these notions develop in his *Phenomenology of Mind, Philosophy of Mind*, and other works.

just outside of the realm of particular determinations. Therefore, they reason, every person is equally abstract, equally self-identical.

Unfortunately, those who reason in this way make one slight error. They forget that "equality" is always a quantitative idea, essentially bound up with quantitative determinations or finite numerical progressions. But if we think of a person as being in some sense situated *outside* quantitative determinations and finite progressions – it would be impossible to apply a quantitative idea such as "equality" to him.

Since we are now situated at the vantage point of the "absolute" will, which, although not immersed in the finite, is nevertheless in dynamic union with the finite, the question of the various possible *relationships* to the finite now emerges. This brings us to a consideration of *property*:

1) Property

The dynamic reciprocal relationship of the "absolute" will to the finite leads in the first instance to the concept of *private property*. For I must *possess* the finite and particular in order to become related to it. And if I begin to derive my sense of personal freedom by relating myself to finite things (external objects) – it is natural that I should begin to keep such finite things around me, in order to perpetuate this experience of personal freedom.

In other words, I must *in some sense* possess a house, to say that my self is related to the house and vice versa. I must possess ideas, to speak about my relationship to them. I must possess my body, in order to enter into a "self-body" relationship. Once I have entered the stage of volitional maturity – absolute will – then the principle prevails: The more finite things I possess, the more possibilities I have for indirectly deriving an experience of my personal freedom

Our relationship to private property, however, can be analyzed into 3 separate moments:*

a) *Coming into possession:* This can take place in various ways: by direct physical grasping of something that has not been claimed by another will; by use or improvement of something which is unclaimed, but is too large or bulky to be seized or grasped by an individual – e.g., a farm or a deposit of iron ore; or by coming to recognize and appreciate for the first time something that one has always "had" but not really possessed (e.g., physical and intellectual capacities that have never been developed).

b) *Using the thing possessed:* If I simply seized something and forgot about

* Hegel designates these moments as three types of "judgement": the positive, negative, and infinite judgment. It is not important for our purposes here to explain this terminology.

it for the rest of my life, my possession of that thing would be open to question. In order to really possess it, I must use it, or change it, or devote it to some purpose. In short, I must in some way give it the stamp of my own personality. Otherwise, it is not really "mine."

c) *Selling or alienating the thing possessed:*

Here there is a paradox. All things considered, there is only one ultimate proof that I own something: namely, my right to sell or dispose of that thing. In thus disposing of my possession, I am affirming (i) that it is something completely external to my personality, and (ii) that I am not immersed in my property, but am able to return periodically into my personality (which amounts indirectly to an act of self-appropriation).

2) *Contract*

Through a relationship to private property, my will becomes related to certain particular, determinate possessions. These possessions, insofar as they are determinate and *limited*, have definite boundary lines, which are borderd by other particular, determinate things. Some of these other things are possessed by other wills, other personalities. Therefore, in a kind of circular fashion, my relationship to particular possessions inevitably brings me into relationships with other persons.

When I come into relationship with another person, it is possible for me to form, with that other person, a "common will" in regard to certain possessions. By mutual agreement, we can make certain decisions about the disposition of property. These decisions result not from my will or his, but from both wills. In other words, we can enter into a "contract."

The term, "*contract*," as used here, refers to all types of alienation of property – whether through gift, or barter, or sale, or legal transaction.

3) *Wrong*

After an individual will has become engaged in contractual relationships with other wills, a new possibility emerges – the possibility of a dispute about property rights.

If no one ever claims a piece of property which I have claimed, the question of right and wrong will never arise. But when others begin to make contradictory or conflicting claims in regard to things I have claimed for myself, I find it necessary to exonerate myself from wrong, and, conversely, to demonstrate that the other person is guilty of wrong.

In order to do this, I must first understand the nature of wrong. I should know, in general, that wrong is the failure to coordinate personal rights ("the universal") with appropriate possessions ("the particular"). A "lack of coordination" can develop in the following three ways:

a) The individual 'does justice" to the universal, but not to the particular. This is *non-malicious wrong*, in which an individual only intends to defend his rights (the universal), but mistakenly claims that certain items of property (the particular) are included with these rights.

b) The individual "does injustice to the universal," by attempting to give the *appearance* of right (the universal) to an action or transaction (the particular) which he knows is wrong. This is what we call *"fraud."*

c) The individual does injustice to the *connection between* universal and particular. In other words, he does not even bother to keep up the appearance of right (as does the defrauder or cheat) – but simply seizes possession of things (the particular), without regard to what is right (the universal). This is what we designate as *"violence" or "crime."*

Another paradox results here:

– This final stage (c) of supreme *wrong* leads indirectly to the emergence of *morality*. For the individual who commits a crime brings retribution upon himself. Other persons, seeing that he has denied or negated the *connection between* universal and particular – are naturally incited to "negate this negation" by punishing the criminal – and thus restore a positive equilibrium in society. In order to mete out punishment justly, however, they must develop the concept of what the connection between the universal and particular is, or "ought" to be. And this is an instigation towards the development of moral theories.

SAMPLE EXAMINATION QUESTIONS

1. In Hegel's chapter on *Property*, a number of paradoxes are to be found: For example, a) my initial psychic "withdrawal" from the external world eventually leads me at the stage of "absolute will," to try to acquire external things; b) my desire for possession of things leads me to sell them or dispose of them; and c) the emergence of violence and crime in society leads to the emergence of morality. Show in more detail how these three paradoxes develop.

SAMPLE ESSAY

Hegel definitely says that our idea of "personality" depends on a relationship to property. Does this insight of Hegel coincide with reality? Is our concept of "personality" defined and differentiated (at least implicitly) by some relationship to private property? It is very important to resolve this problem; since, if personality is *essentially* related to property, it would seem to be implied that those lacking in property would be "un-persons," in a sense.

Part II. MORALITY

In the preceding section the absolute will was "immediately" related to the finite (i.e. finite objects). In the stage which we are about to consider, the absolute will enters into a "mediated" relationship – i.e. a relationship mediated by its own subjective but universal *concepts*.

At the end of the last section on "Wrong," we saw that wrong (unjust seizure of property, etc.) indirectly leads to the emergence of universal concepts about right and wrong. For when we are faced with disputes and conflicting claims, we need to develop universal criteria which can be applied to such cases, enabling us to make decisions about what "ought "to be done. These criteria are moral norms.

Moral norms go beyond rights. If, for example, I have a "right" to a farm, this means 1) that I am related to a certain external *object*; and 2) that I can utilize and develop and *form* this object as I like. But morality is not related to particular objects, but rather to universal *objectives*, or purposes. And morality is not interested in impressing this or that particular form upon the external world, but with bringing into existence its universal *concepts* (putting moral ideals into practice).

But the universal objectives or purposes to wh'ch the moral will is directed, come *within* persons, from subjective thought. And the universal concepts or moral ideals which are created by the moral will are not external creations but *internal*, subjective creations. Therefore we can say that the moral will in a very real sense "determines itself," i.e., is self-determined. And since it is one thing for a personality to determine external reality (this is the primary concern of the absolute will in its immediate stage) and quite another thing to *be* determinate, i.e. to determine oneself as an object – it is only with the arrival of the moral will that the will's power of self-determination becomes truly explicit ("for-itself").

Let us go on to consider moral *activity*, by analyzing it in terms of its antitheses:

First antithesis: subjective purpose vs. responsibility:

When we develop moral purposes, and try to put them into *effect*, we encounter a twofold limitation: a) we have a limited knowledge of the circumstances in our environment; and b) we have a limited knowledge of possible consequences of our activity. Because of these limitations, the question of *responsibility* emerges as a counterbalance to our moral judgments: If I didn't know the gun was loaded, I may have little or no responsibility for killing someone with it. If someone commits suicide as a result of misunderstanding my non-malicious statement, my responsibility for his suicide is minimal or nil.

Second antithesis: intention vs. welfare:

The subjective purposes which we try to express in our moral activity have two aspects: a) They are *universal intentions*, supposedly applicable to each and every person, provided that he finds himself in comparable circumstances; b) they are particular goals, designed to contribute to the happiness or *welfare* of *particular* individuals. Thus morality itself has a twofold connotation: a) it connotes altruism, sacrifice, and the sense of duty; and b) it connotes self-fullfillment and the pursuit of happiness. In the context of social interaction, these two aspects develop in the form of a basic conflict between a) the common good (moral duty) and b) individual fulfillment (moral right).

Third antithesis: Good vs. conscience:

We have just discussed the basic conflict that develops between moral duties and moral rights. Confronted with this conflict, the moral will decides that it is necessary to maintain a constant balance or equilibrium in the objective sphere (society) between "the universal" (duties) and "the particular" (rights). *This objective balance* or equilibrium is what we mean by "*Good.*"

But objective good gives rise to its own antithesis – subjective *conscience*. For the good (the objective equilibrium between rights and duties) is not found ready-made in the world. It must be determined and created by individual conciousnesses, i.e., by *consciences*. But since the subjective is in opposition to the objective, a continual conflict between conscience and "the good" results. Thus a paradoxical situation develops: Conscience, in a very real sense, creates objective good; but finds itself continually at odds with the good that has been created (by others, or even by itself).

– This latter paradox leads us to a significant problem: Can we not conceive of a situation in which what is "good" in the objective social milieu is fully determined *by the individual consciences* of the members of that milieu; and in which, conversely, the individual consciences participating in a society (finding their own concept of "good" reflected in that society) allow themselves to be determined *by the objective good* recognized in that society.

– This conception of an ideal rapport between the individual determinant will and his objective moral world is called the *"Ethical Life."* It is a vague conception which gradually begins to take on form in the sections that follow.

SAMPLE EXAMINATION QUESTIONS

1. Contrast a) "right" with "morality"; b) "duty" with "happiness"; and c) "the good" with "conscience." Show in what sense each of these antitheses is an illustration of the fundamental opposition between objectivity and subjectivity, or between universality and particularity.

TERM PAPER TOPIC

Hegel's critique of Kant's notion of "morality." When Hegel describes the antithesis of "duty vs. happiness," he is referring especially to the Kantian notion of morality. Kant develops this antithesis in the second section of *Fundamental Principles of a Metaphysics of Morals* (Liberal Arts Library). Analyze Kant's references to "duty" and "happiness" in this second section to determine whether Hegel's depiction of the Kantian antithesis is accurate. For an extensive comparison of Hegelian and Kantian ethics, see W. H. Walsh, *Hegelian Ethics* (St. Martin's Press).

In the history of philosophy, an interesting antithesis to the Kantian emphasis on duty is found in J. S. Mill's utilitarian ethic. See, for example, Mill's short essay, *Utilitarianism.*

Part III. ETHICAL LIFE

During the stage of "morality" (see the preceding section), the individual becomes primarily interested in setting up "oughts" for himself and others. If he measures up to these "oughts" to some degree, he attains a certain satisfaction. He has the experience of actually determining himself. And since the power of self-determination, without dependence on external circumstances, is generally considered to be an aspect of freedom – the experience of self-determination is an experience of personal *freedom*.

However, morality is in a certain sense deficient or even bad. The individual who is characterized by a moral will can attain to a sense of freedom only at a price. The price he must pay is a feeling of alienation from his external, objective social circumstances. The moral will develops a need to negate *de facto* human behavior. It does this by creating pure ideals, or "oughts," which stand in stark contrast to real behavior, and put this behavior in a "bad light." If real behavior "shapes up," so to speak, if it is brought into closer conformity with moral ideals – the "moral" individual is still not satisfied. He is primarily interested only in showing that his "oughts" are independent from reality (*self*-determined). Therefore he develops a psychic need to continually find something wrong with reality, something which "ought not" to be.

The moral will, as a "subjective" manifestation of absolute will, strove for a primarily subjective reconciliation of the universal and the particular. But the objective world (naturally) failed to reflect the subjective reconciliations which were being attempted. Therefore the moral will continually fell back upon itself, alienated, feeling the full pessimism of the ought. In order to get beyond this impasse, two things must take place: a) the individual conscience must cease to look upon objectivity as something "out there," which must be forced into conformity with the norms of conscience: b) "objective good," on its side, must cease to be an abstraction or a utopian ideal, capable of realization in the future; it must be presented in its full concreteness – as the rational kernel of presently existing persons and institutions, and the customs and laws governing the interrelationships of these persons and institutions. When this final phase is reached, the union of the particular and the universal which characterizes the absolute will, is no longer merely an "in-itself," as it is in abstract right, where the immediate relationship of persons and property is paramount; nor is it merely "for-itself," as it was in the extremely subjective phase of morality: but it is "in-and-for-itself," i.e. immediate and at the same time mediated by thought, objective and at the same time completely imbued with subjectivity, fluid and indeterminate and yet at the same time determined and controlled by subjectivity, passively determined and yet at the same time actively self-determining (since it is composed of self-determining conscious agents).

This final phase of the absolute will, this perfection of absolute freedom, is obviously a parodoxical entity. Where is it to be found? In the appearance of "Ethical Life."

*Ethical life** develops in three distinct spheres, which will be considered in the following sections:

1) *The Family*, the nuclear prototype of mutual voluntary submission.

2) *"Civil Society,"* the socio-economic sphere in which there is a paradoxical conflict-and-harmony of individual will and social will.

3) *The State*, which brings about a final constructive opposition among the various participants in ethical existence.

TERM PAPER TOPIC

The Hegelian ideal of "ethical" existence.
J. Glen Gray has written a short book, *Hegel and Greek Thought* (Harper Torchbooks), in which he shows that Hegel's notion of "ethical life" is based on the model of the Greek city-state.

Consult this book with the following question in mind: Why does Hegel consider "ethical life" (*Sittlichkeit*, as exemplified in the Greek city-state) to be a higher stage than "morality"?

---

* Hegel differentiates 'ethical" from "moral." "Moral" for Hegel connotes an "abstract and subjective viewpoint"; while "ethical" implies the "concrete" embodiment, in various ways, of subjective human freedom in multifarious aspects of objective existence.

Sub-section 1 THE FAMILY

The absolute will, as we have seen, establishes, for the first time, a real union and rapport between the subjective will and "objectivity." In the third and final phase of absolute will, "objectivity" becomes more specifically defined as man's social and political environment.

The union or rapport which results in this case is an explicit manifestation of Spirit.* Spirit, in all of its forms, is a union of opposites. At the present stage, its first explicit manifestation is the union of natural opposites (male and female) through natural attraction ("self-feeling," or love). Thus the ethical institution of the family, inevitably resulting from this natural attraction, is a kind of groundwork or basis for all the ramifications of ethical life in society.

We will discuss the family in terms of the following three stages:

A. The stage of love and marriage
B. The stage of property and capital
C. The stage of dissolution

A. The stage of love and marriage

Spirit, as a unity of opposites, is based on life (which has given rise to spirit). Human love and marriage is a peculiar case where spirit and life reflect each other perfectly, so that it is difficult to distinguish them from each other.

Life, at a certain level of perfection, breaks up into the polarities of "male" and "female," in order to bring about higher and more complex types of unity. Spirit, corresponding to life, also breaks up into a polarity of two opposite personality characteristics – existence-in-self** (which ordinarily characterizes the female) and existence-for-self** (which ordinarily characterizes the male). "Existence-in-self" implies an immediate sense of self-unity, and a mind and will which is oriented towards particularity and individuality.

---

* See glossary for the special Hegelian meaning of this word. Also, it should be noted that in many English translations of Hegel, "mind" is used instead of "spirit."
** See glossary, p. 12 ff.

'Existence-for-self," on the other hand, implies a self-reflection of personality, and an orientation towards universality (which is always produced by
a reflection on particulars).

Marriage is thus a state in which the natural polarization of life into male
and female generally coincides with, and fosters, the polarization of spirit
into masculine and feminine personality characteristics.

Insofar as marriage involves a physical union, it is based on contingencies, –
sexual attraction, the moment of romantic love, etc. In our days, these contingencies have assumed the aspect of supreme importance – and, if we are
to take contemporary drama as a witness, the whole structure of love and
marriage must stand or fall on the basis of romantic feelings. But this is to
give undue emphasis to the physical and passional elements of love, which
are sublimated in marriage.

Insofar as marriage is a personal union of the existence-in-self of the female
with the existence-for-self of the male, it involves a free, subjective transaction which is at the same time objective and "universal" (because it is based
on natural attraction, and thus is not completely under the control of an
individual's subjective will).

In its essence, marriage is the mutual sacrifice of one's personality to another, for the purpose of finding oneself in a higher sense. It is not a contract,
since it is a *sacrifice* of individual rights.* Rather, you could say more accur-
ately that it is a "contract to do away with contracts" – i.e., a "contract" to
enter into a union of love in which questions of a contractual nature will
never enter. Because its essence is to get beyond the sphere of personal unity to
create a new unity – marriage is essentially mongamous and indissoluble (since
polygamy would imply that a married person still *had* rights over his personality, and divorce implies much the same thing).

The personal (ethical) aspect of a marriage is the factor which takes marriage out of the contingent sphere of physical passion, and gives it stability.
Hence this aspect is more important, and should precede considerations of
physical attraction. However, it can also be overemphasized – e.g., in societies which are regulated by "arranged" marriages, etc.

The ancient "*household gods*" (*Penates*) are symbols of the new and higher
"personality" which is created by marriage.

"*Platonic*" love (including monasticism,** etc.) is an attempt to acquire the

---

* A contract is never a sacrifice of rights, but only an exchange of rights, or a mutual
compromise in regard to rights.

** Monasticism is "Platonic" love in the sense that the monk strives to acquire a
"mystical" union with God. Other forms of Platonic love are attempts to achieve a purely
spiritual union with a person of the opposite sex.

spiritual aspect of marital union, in exclusion from the physical. But the indirect effect of this is to give exaggerated emphasis to the physical, as something "other" and mysterious.

The religious or civil ceremony constitutes the formal completion and actuality of the "marriage contract to end all contracts." Like many other contracts, it brings about what it symbolizes.

Marriages between close relatives are contrary to the requirement that two distinctive, unique personalities should enter marriage. An initial opposition and distinctiveness is necessary, if the dynamism of life is to be maximally creative.

B. Family capital

Insofar as the family is a complex, universal, and enduring "personality," it requires something more than "property" in its ordinary sense as its external embodiment. It requires property which has an aura of permanence and stability – property which we might designate as capital, or estate.

The family capital is a common possession, even though it is administered by the husband, even though differences may arise among family members about its administration, and even though the state may make various laws governing its distribution in case of death, divorce, etc.

Finally, just as the family, in more advanced societies has a self-subsistence over against the "house" (tribe or clan) of the husband or wife – so also the family property is substantially connected with the family, and only accidentally related to the sphere of possession of the clan or "house."

C. The education of children and the dissolution of the family

Children are the only *external*, existent objectification of that internal, subjective feeling of love which supplies the basis for the family as an ethical unity. In other words, if it were not for children, the familial Penates and the love of the parents would always remain merely subjective or ideal unities – and for that reason vague unities.

Since these children are potentially free, they can never be considered as slaves (in contrast to Roman law). The whole orientation of the parents should be to help the child through love and discipline, and common capital – to attain to the status of freedom (and, paradoxically, to their separation from family unity). (N.B. the indulgent and permissive "play theory" of education which is currently* popular ignores the necessity of giving children an aspiration to grow up, i.e., to be dissatisfied with their childish activities).

---

* In Hegel's time.

Insofar as the feelings of the parents are a contingent type of "fact" – they are subject to alteration. Thus *divorce* is always a possibility. But the state should possess procedures for helping the couple to distinguish between real emotional alienation and temporary whims and disgruntlement.

Insofar as the death of the parents (especially the father) creates a natural break-up of the family – the laws must make provisions for the inheritance of common property. But an individual father can impede these laws – for example, by willing his estate to a circle of friends or acquaintances, on the ground that these are a "moral" family. This "moral" family seems to take precedence, especially after the dissolution of the natural family through the father's death. The ethical title to property in such cases is often extremely vague.

Such arbitrary actions on the part of the father could obviously be justified if his wife and all his children were deceased; or perpaps even if the family ties had become extremely remote, through divorce, long absence, etc.

But if the wife and/or children were still living, and if there were some substantial family ties – the father, in making a whimsical will, would be implicitly depending on those members whom he is *disinheriting* to respect his wishes. This would be an obvious self-contradiction – to ask for respect from those whose respect and opinions you implicitly hold in contempt.

In most cases, such actions are simply forceful and poignant "proofs" of the fact that marriage as an *immediate* ethical stage, is a necessary institution based on the *natural contingencies* of feeling.

In our civil laws, we must be careful to avoid placing so much importance on these contingent aspects that they begin to obscure the essential ethical nature of marriage. Otherwise, we will find ourselves in the shoes of the legalists of the Roman empire, who, in order to satisfy individual whims, admitted that sons were slaves of the father, and that the wife in certain cases (when she was classified as the *materfamilias*) was a slave – and then tried to counterbalance the inequity of their laws through compromising judicial interpretations. Or we will end up like the English, who are notorious for allowing every kind of whim and eccentricity in a man's last will and testament.

The general principle we should remember is this: When a man makes an arbitrary will, he is simply showing preference for outsiders rather than his family, or for certain members of his family rather than others. But the family, as a necessary ethical institution must be preferred and fostered in preference to the arbitrary preferences of the father.

SAMPLE EXAMINATION QUESTIONS

1. Hegel sees marriage as a result of a "collusion" between natural organic "Life" and conscious "Spirit." Show how he comes to this conclusion.
2. What value judgements does Hegel make about a) divorce, b) polygamy, and c) consanguineous marriages?
3. In what sense might it be a self-contradiction for a father to ask that his family be disinherited after his death?

ESSAY TOPIC

Marriage gives new meaning to the terms, "personality," "contract," and "property."

Compare these new meanings (*Philosophy of Right*, paragraphs 163, 170 and 171) with the former meaning of these terms (*Philosophy of Right*, paragraphs 35–39, 41–42, 46, and 72–75).

TERM PAPER SUGGESTIONS

1. *Hegel on the nature of woman.* For a more detailed "phenomenological" analysis of the nature of woman, see Hegel's *Phenomenology of Mind* (Baillie translation, pp. 474–478), in which Hegel chooses the tragic figure of Sophocles' Antigone as his model.

For an introduction to the context of this section of the Phenomenology, see Findlay, *Hegel: a Re-examination* (Collier books), Ch. 5, or Kaufman, *Hegel: a Re-interpretation* (Weiderfeld and Nicolson), Section 30.

2. *Reactions to Hegel's concept of the nature of woman.* Kierkegaard makes frequent use of Hegel's "metaphysical" distinction of woman in terms of "existence-in-self." For examples of this, see my article, "The Relationship of Dread to Spirit in Man and Woman, according to Kierkegaard," in *The Modern Schoolman* XLVII, 1, Nov. 1969 pp. 1–13.

Simone de Beauvoir reacts negatively to the rationalistic Hegelian approach in *The Second Sex* (Bantam Books, pp. xvii, 7, 59, and elsewhere (see Index)). According to her, Hegel's existence-in-self would make woman into a mere object, an "other,"* completely outside the domain of free selfhood (i.e. existence-for-self, which is a male prerogative). For a brief analysis of Beauvoir's interpretation, see my article, "A non-Marxian Application of Hegel's Master-Slave Dialectic to some Contemporary Politico-Social Problems," in *Idealistic Studies* III, 3, Sept. 1973.

Show by the use of texts how two opposite currents of existentialism (represented by de Beauvoir and by Kierkegaard, respectively) react to the Hegelian notion that woman represents "existence-in-self."

---

* This would be in terms of the dialectic of *Spirit*. See p. 8 of my introduction.

Sub-section 2. CIVIL SOCIETY

Civil Society results from the further explicit emergence of the "concrete"*
person, who is a concrete unity of natural necessity and capricious freedom
(Wilkur), of means and end (such that the individual person takes himself as
his own end, and as the means to attain his "ends").** It is the realm where
each individual "Burgher" is explicitly striving only to fulfill his own needs
and wants, but is inevitably led (by *necessity*) to participate in the *system* of
needs obtaining among all diverse individuals. Thus it is the sphere in which
particularity asserts itself explicitly, as an unending spiral of accidental and
"natural" needs, which are interconnected into infinity – and finally require
the intervention of universality (in the form of political control) to give them
the form of rationality and spiritual harmony. In other words, particularity
leads into universality by *necessity* here – and not freely.

*According to the requirements of the "Idea"** civil society is naturally *prior*
to the emergence of the state, insofar as differentiation is naturally prior to
unity-in-differentiation.

Historically speaking, however, civil society may be temporally *posterior*
to some immediate state-unity. For example, the ancient monolithic states
which were based on religious or ethnic unity (e.g., the Babylonian empire);
or on an intellectual unity (e.g., the pre-Socratic Greek model). In such cases,
the emergence of civil society presents itself as a threat to harmony, and brings
forth counterbalancing measures (e.g., in Plato's "*Republic*" in which individual aspirations and private property were to be subordinated to an extreme
type of political unity).

In the *world-historical* context, *Christianity* and *Roman citizenship* were the
main milestones by which individual freedom began to assert its rights over
such monolithic states.

The purpose of education must be formulated in accord with the Idea,

---

* See glossary.
** See the earlier section on Private Property, in which "personality" is defined.

which balances immediate* unity with "mediated" differentiation. Those who overemphasize immediate unity yearn for the restoration of some abstract and fictional "state of nature," and are forced into the logical conclusion of regarding education as superfluous. Those who overemphasize mediated differentiation look upon education simply as a means of learning to attain individual desires more effectively. *True* education should recognize explicitly that the highest unity is the unity of free individuals, but also that individual desires are chaotic and self-defeating unless they become attuned to the universal goals of the community.

The stages of the development of "civil society" are as follows:

A. the development of the *system of needs* in the social sphere;

B. the development of a *system of justice* to protect individuals in obtaining their needs;

C. the development of organized *police* and organized *corporations* to protect people against contingencies lurking in each of the preceding "systems."

A. The system of needs

Subjective need, which becomes emphasized in the sphere of "civil society," is a) directly oriented to *external objects* (the immediate objective goal of subjective needs) and b) indirectly oriented to *work* (the means of attaining or producing the needed external objects). This process of orientation develops into a "system of needs." The political economists (Adam Smith, Say, Ricardo, etc.) exert laudable efforts to focus on "necessary" relationships amidst the contingencies of this "system." But they operate from the finite vantage point of the Understanding,* while our concern here is to treat the same subject matter from the vantage point of Reason (the speculative unity of opposites).

1) The development of need and satisfaction into "genera" (§§ 190–195): *"Man"* in the primary and most appropriate usage of that term refers to the free individual in the context of civil society, where the primal distinction of human beings from brute animals becomes apparent (namely, the ability of men to get beyond restricted "natural" needs, by differentiating and universalizing and categorizing needs).

The differentiating of needs by man in civil society a) takes place by a process of abstraction, which begins from various natural needs, and proceeds to abstract various aspects of these needs and correlate abstract natural

* See glossary.

needs and aspects of natural needs with other needs and aspects of needs; b) results in an infinite possibility of multiplication of external needs, along with the infinite impossibility of ever satisfying them; and c) brings about social sensitivity, since (i) needs are concerned with external objects subject to *appropriation* by *others*, and (ii) abstract and artificial needs are needs which can only be *recognized* and appreciated by other men.

"*Refinement*" is the ability of discerning and evaluating needs, and inter-relating them. *Luxury* is the process of multiplying needs *ad infinitum* – a process which leads inevitably to artificially-induced want, deprivation, and depravity.

2) The development of work into "genera" (§§ 196–198):

The work of acquiring and producing external objects takes place by *methods* which become diversified in the same way that needs and objects become diversified. When these diverse *methods* assume an importance of their own, man becomes oriented primarily to *commodities* – i.e., external objects whose value results primarily from the fact that they are produced by diverse human methods.

The diversification of methods of working upon objects, results in the "division of labor" and the specialization and mechanization of labor (which will indirectly result in the production of specialized *machines* to free man from labor).

Education in a "working" society involves a) the theoretical ability to deal with a multiplicity of abstract ideas, and to vary and interrelate these ideas with facility and adaptability; b) the practical orientation to *work* itself, as a means of expressing or objectifying oneself in set, publicly recognized ways. (N.B. as regards this "practical" education, it would be quite true to say that education in a working society is essentially education to *work* – something that is universally lacking in savages).

3) Resources (§§ 199–208):

The interdependence of the various spheres of labor is represented by capital – the universal means by which products and needs are translated from one form into another.

The various need-systems, however, do not become a simple unity under the insignia of capital; but rather they become diversified into more or less stable clusters, giving rise to *social classes*.

The social classes which develop under the influence of capital, can be grouped into three main and essential divisions, in accord with the dialectic of the Idea*:

* See glossary for the Hegelian meaning of "Idea."

a) *The agricultural class*, which represents civil society in its "immediate" form. The agricultural class represents the first emergence from undiversified nomadic existence. Agricultural existence brings with it not only the maintenance of private property, but also the stabilization of sexuality into marriage, and of possessions into common family capital. However, this form of existence is "immediate," insofar as it is tied to the soil and the bounty of nature. Reflection (i.e., "mediation") enters in only in the form of provision for the future. Freedom and the bid for human control enter into agricultural existence only in a minimal way.

b) *The business class*, which gets beyond the nature-oriented immediacy of agricultural existence, and introduces a type of existence which is dependent mostly on human reflection, and the power of man to give *form* to raw materials. This class, because of its emphasis on man's power over matter, is notable for its emphasis on law and order and morality as the explicit manifestations of man's freedom.*

The three main groupings of the business class are
   (i) *Craftsmen*, who are concerned with forming single objects to satisfy single needs.
  (ii) *Manufacturers*, who produce supplies to meet more universal demands – and thus engage in a more abstract or universal type of production.
 (iii) *Merchants*, who engage in the exchange of commodities through the use of *money* (which actualizes the abstract "monetary" value of commodities and allows them to be traded more easily).

c) *The bureaucracy*, made up of civil servants who work for the universal interests of society. The bureaucracy, more than the other two classes, should be devoid of the temptation to acquire illegal profits, accept bribes, etc. Therefore, as a rule, bureaucrats should be either independently wealthy or substantially remunerated from the public treasury.

Existence in, or entrance into, a particular social class is inevitably determined by "accidental" factors – capital resources that an individual has inherited or been endowed with, without earning them; physical and mental abilities; favorable circumstances for achieving various peaks of performance, skill, and success. However, amidst all these "necessary contingencies," there is still room, at least in Western society, for the operation of freedom. (In societies which stifle individual initiative by relegating class divisions to accidents of nature – for example, ancient Sparta, or nineteenth-century India – these class divisions inevitably appear in their true light, as something

---

* Freedom here, of course, means freedom from immersion in, and subjection to, matter.

hostile, i.e., as a false type of individuation which has not been properly assimilated by the free members of the society in question.)

The *"equality of men"* is an artificial and mythical concept, produced by an abstraction from really existent men. The fact is, men are inherently unequal both in their endowments and in the way they use these endowments. And if one refuses to particularize and differentiate himself in the sphere of "inequalities," not only will he fail to attain his abstract ideal of equality, but he will also fail to actualize his freedom.

– *The transition to Justice:*

The right to property, which has been the basic principle in the whole development of the system of needs, becomes explicit with the emergence of social classes, – and leads to the *administration of justice* (which is concerned with the protection of property rights).

B. The administration of justice

The right of property, as the implicit principle of the system of needs, became expressed as the infinite reciprocity of needs-and-work (an abstract expression of personality in the socio-economic sphere). When this infinite reciprocity becomes explicit through education, and thus appears as the universal law governing the relationship between particular persons, it becomes something actually existent in the world and objective to consciousness – i.e., the administration of justice. The principle of justice begins to fashion all persons in the state into a single, "universal" person, without, however, leading them on to "cosmopolitanism."

1) The process by which right becomes law (§§ 211–214):

In any society with a minimum of culture the recognition of "rights" is implicit in the national mores; in the unwritten laws which give national unity to a people; and also in moral laws (but only insofar as these moral laws go beyond private and subjective behavior, and have a bearing on objective civil rights).

All these rights become explicit in law (*Gesetz*), which – as is indicated from its very etymology* – has to do essentially with the act of positing rights. Hence the law that we are concerned with here is essentially "positive" law.

Positive law is not a determination of what "ought" to be, but is merely the interpretation of what the mores or morals of a society are, and the application of these mores or morals to concrete situations. In this process of interpretation and application, which is an operation of *thought*, the laws cease

---

* *Gesetz* in German is derived from a word which means "to set down" or to "posit."

to be vague and ambiguous, and take on the aspect of *universality* and *determinateness* (universality because of the presence of thought, determinateness because of the application to concrete situations). It is possible, of course, that there may be misinterpretations as to what the mores or morals actually *are*, in a given positive application. But we must not go to the extreme of refusing to trust anyone to make such applications. (There are some currents of thought which are appalled at the realization that in positive law-making we have to enter the quantitative sphere, considering not only "examples" but actual *cases*, and making quantitative determinations as to the number of days to be spent in jail, etc. This, they say, is the sphere of irrationality and contingency. And they are correct in saying this. But it is also the function of reason to know its own limitations, and to stop short of trying to make everything rational. It is absolutely necessary that we take the chance of making misapplications, and of contributing to judicial clashes – if we are ever to progress in the process of applying and adjudicating the law – i.e., of making the law explicit.)

We should also try to avoid the extreme that the English go to, with their "unwritten laws," to avoid misapplications and conflicting interpretations. As it turns out, the English system is based on a whole host of court decisions which serve as precedents – which places the judge in the unenviable position of having to decide whether the "unwritten law" is written down in the precedents, or exists within his own heart.

The science of positive law has chiefly to do with the history of legal rights and the continuity of authority in a given society. Over and above this, the Understanding may go on to classify and make deductions from laws. But if it goes so far as to try to discern necessary *laws for* the application or "positing" *of laws* – it gets involved in the fictions of the imagination.

2) *The process by which law becomes existent* (§§ 215–218):

Law which is posited in a given society can become effectively existent only if it is promulgated (since every person has a fundamental right to know what is right).

"*Promulgation*" does not imply an elaboration of all details of applicability of a law. This, of course, would be to seek for infinity in the sphere of the infinite – which would be ridiculous. But in law, as in science and philosophy, it is possible to set down at least all the *essential* universal principles – and this is what is required. Those who say that law is something only for experts and completely outside the competency of the layman – would have to say with equal logic that a customer has no right to judge whether the shoe salesman has given him the right size of shoe.

A complete code of law, then, should be promulgated. But if a code of law is complete, and is couched in an ancient classical language or technical jargon, or written on musty tombstones – it might as well not be promulgated at all. And so we must add the further stipulation that the law is effectively promulgated only when it is publicly accessible and publicly known.

Property transactions (after law becomes "existent" in the aforementioned sense) should be accompanied by the proper attitude towards *formalities*. Ceremonies and formalities should not, of course, be looked upon as ends in themselves. But nevertheless, the observance of modern and up-to-date *forms* of property transfer must take precedence over ancient property titles or abstract considerations of right and wrong.

Crime, in the context of adequately existent positive law, ceases to be a merely subjective offense* and takes on further aspects of quantitative and qualitative damage to society, which may increase the gravity of the offense (for example, stealing a few pennies may be a crime punishable by death in an incipient and very unstable society). But paradoxically, these further aspects may also serve to decrease the magnitude of a crime (for example, stealing a hundred dollars may be considered a very minor crime in a relatively stable and affluent society).

3) The process by which existent law vindicates itself through judgments (§§ 219–229):

After right becomes determined as positive law, and after positive law becomes "existent" through proper promulgation, there is still one further step necessary: namely, that positive law, which has become, as it were, a self-subsistent entity in a society, should vindicate its universal validity in the *processes of legal judgment*, and thus also meet the demands of human self-consciousness, which has an inalienable right to know its rights.

The processes of judgment, which should be initiated and carried out under the direction of a judge, are as follows:

a) *The process of inquiry:* This is an investigation often carried out by a jury, and has to do with the facts pertinent to a case – e.g., whether a crime has been committed, what is the precise nature of the crime, etc.

The process of ascertainment here is largely a matter of subjective certainty about empirical facts. The adjudicator is striving for subjective certainty about the facts. The "facts" are circumstances which give evidence of the subjective intentions of the defendant. Included among these circumstances

---

* I.e. a "negatively infinite" judgment, a judgment which denies the essential infinite reciprocity between a person and his property rights. See the preceeding remarks about "violence," p. 21.

are the oaths of witnesses, which are also enunciations of *their* subjective certainty.

Thus to a great extent, this process is the investigation by the judge of subjective certainties of witnesses about the subjective intentions of the defendant, for the purpose of himself arriving at subjective certainty regarding the presence or absence of guilt, etc.

Although such an inquiry could perhaps be carried out with equal or better proficiency by legal experts, it is a healthy custom for it to be carried out by a group of laymen who are peers of the defendant (as is the general rule in German law). If this is not done, the judgment rendered would come from some foreign, external body, and the rights of freedom and self-consciousness to be its own judge (at least vicariously, through its peers) would not be preserved.

b) *The stages of legal action:* It is important that these steps be just as clearly defined as the laws which they are meant to implement. It is also absolutely necessary that they be made public. If either of these prerequisites were lacking, the "promulgation" of the law would be lacking its proper logical conclusion; and the rights of self-consciousness to have complete knowledge of the law would be infringed upon.

The purpose of these clearly-defined steps of legal action is to make possible an objective and publicly ascertainable proof of guilt, innocence, etc. This is not to ignore the fact that a person may be innocent without being able to prove his innocence. But unprovable innocence is something completely outside the sphere of law.

Because the complexity of such steps, and the need for objective proof, can very often thwart, rather than promote, the cause of justice, *courts of equity* have been established, with the power to do away with such proceedings and even with the requirements of proof, when the nature of the case permits it.

c) *The process of legal judgment:* In German law, this is usually the prerogative of a judge. In rendering judgment, he has a duty to show the relationship of a particular case to the law, and also to relate that particular case correctly to the relevant law or laws.

If this judgment has been preceded by a *trial by jury*, the judgement is called an "extraordinary" judgment.

If punishment is inflicted, the infliction of the punishment has certain implications: a) *Subjectively*, it implies that the defendant is restoring law within himself (this implication is especially manifest when the defendant has been judged by his peers, i.e., other "selves"); b) *Objectively*, it implies that the law is vindicating itself, and being restored to itself by annulling the public crime publicly through the stipulated punishment.

– Transition to the Police and the Corporation

Getting beyond the administration of justice in isolated particular cases, we have now to consider how this administration is extended *over the whole realm of particularity* 1) in a relative way, by the police; and 2) in a more perfect way, by the corporation.

*C. The police and the corporation**

1) The police (public authority)

As civil society develops, its main interest is to facilitate the interconnection of needs, and to arrange for quicker and more certain sat·sfaction of these needs. To accomplish this interest, it develops various means of communication for interconnecting needs and resources, and also develops generalized or standardized processes for supplying needs. But as indirect results of these processes, various contingencies develop: Work becomes specialized so much that certain elements of society are dehumanized; the interests of producer and consumer come into conflict; families are uprooted, and individuals are thrown into an industrial milieu where the law is "every man for himself"; grave imbalances in the distribution of wealth develop, and the impoverished masses are spurred on by environmental circumstances to laziness and/or crime; and so forth.

The public authority, or police, enters into this picture as the means for securing the interests of the universal, amidst all these contingencies. Its aim, so to speak, is to keep particularity under control. Its justification is the everpresent possibility of wrong, i.e., the transgression of particular rights.

The public authority achieves its universal aim by various means.

a) by fixing prices on certain goods which are necessary for public subsistence;

b) By public control of industries whose stability and equilibrium are most necessary for public welfare, or whose conduct of its very nature brings society into the area of internat·onal trade (something too complex to be left to individual interests);

c) By instituting extreme measures of control, at times of crisis or emergency;

* Hegel means something quite different by "police" and "corporation" than we do, as will become clear in the following section.

At this point, Hegel's description of two main types of corporation may help: "A corporation...comprises all who ply the same trade in a town, and it has the right that any society has of admitting whom it will and excluding anyone who does not conform to its rules... The members of every branch of learned study have [also] united into a corporation..." (*Positivity of Christian Religion*, § 22.)

"Police" (*Polizei*), according to Hegel, is related in signification to the Greek word, πολῖτέια, "public authority."

d) By creating public charitable institutions (hospitals, orphanages, etc.), so that the contingency of individual benevolence will not be overwhelmed by the contingencies of need;

e) By alleviating the needs of the poor, so as to prevent the creation of an impoverished rabble, or slums. Since civil society has loosened family solidarity (which was a form of insurance against poverty) and since poverty breeds laziness and crime – civil society has both a duty and a need to protect itself against this situation. It may do this (i) by grants (derived from taxes levied on the rich, or by seeking assistence from the endowments of rich hospitals, etc.) or (ii) by artificially creating jobs. The first alternative has the disadvantage of failing to instill the self-respect requisite for a member of civil society; the second has the disadvantage of setting up imbalances in production, etc. It is up to the public authority to balance these two disadvantages against each other, in a continual dialectic.

f) By controlling education through public funds – since uncertainty of education is another by-product of the dissolution of family ties produced by civil society.

g) By undertaking and overseeing or at least facilitating, the emigration of colonists overseas. This "external" function of the public authority is an exemplification of the fact that the expansion of civil society is naturally connected with the sea, just as the expansion of the family was naturally connected with the land. But it is also a necessity, in view of the "dialectic" mentioned in e); for the instability of economic fluctuations at home inevitably leads nations to look for outlets abroad to which they may send their unemployed.

2) *The corporation* (i.e., not only business corporations, but also labor federations and professional societies).

In the corporation, the constant oppositions a) of natural ability versus material rewards, and b) of abstract right versus abstract self-interest – are finally reconciled. For a) the corporation is a civil "family," which gives the guarantee of material security to those who have certain abilities, and become members; and b) the corporation also raises the pursuit of individual welfare to the level of a *right*.

The origin of the corporation, philosophically speaking, is the fact that the splintering process which takes place in civil society inevitably produces diverse genera of particular interests which coincide within each genus. Thus those who pursue a similar profession or trade band together for their mutual protection and advancement, and the "corporation" results.

Some of the *aims* of the corporation are as follows: To set up standards for proficiency in a certain profession; to educate neophytes, and accept or reject aspirants for membership; to guarantee that the poorer members should receive assistance from the richer; to direct natural skills in accord with the "artificial" contingencies of the laws of economics; to regulate the size of the membership, in such a way that all may be secured against unemployment.

– *Transition to the State:*

The family, rooted in agricultural existence, gave birth to civil society, which was rooted in, and identified with, the town. As town life developed and differentiated itself, the differentiation of universal from particular also became explicit. The defense of particularity through universality became embodied in the police (public authority), while the ascendancy of particular interest to universal interests became exemplified in the corporation (which, from our point of view – the viewpoint of particularity – constitutes the second "ethical basis" for the state after the family).

But the public authority is an "external" type of universal, and the corporation represents only a partial and restricted reconciliation of the particular with the universal. What is needed is a more internally conditioned type of universality; and a more comprehensive union of particularity with the universal. And both of these requisites are to be found in the *state*.

SAMPLE EXAMINATION QUESTIONS

1. In what sense is "civil society" prior to the state? In what sense is it posterior to the state?
2. Hegel says that civil society is "a spectacle of extravagance and want" (*Philosophy of Right*, p. 185). What does he mean by this? Comment.
3. Does Hegel view Plato as a propagonist for, or an antagonist against, freedom? Explain.
4. According to Hegel, the differentiation of man from the lower animals becomes apparent in civil society. How does he come to this conclusion?
5. What are the 3 main "class divisions" in civil society? What is the primary source or cause for these class divisions, in Hegel's view?
6. According to some people, law should have nothing to do with determining quantitative "contingencies" – e.g. how many days a wrongdoer should spend in jail. How does Hegel argue *against* this position?
7. Hegel suggests that there are two primary means for combating poverty in society. What are they? What are the merits and deficiencies of each of these means, in Hegel's estimation?

TERM PAPER TOPICS

1. *The meaning of "civil society" in Hegel's political philosophy.*
M. B. Foster, in *The Political Philosophies of Plato and Hegel*) (N.Y.: Russell and Russell, 1965) devotes one chapter to analyzing the historical development of the notion of "civil society" which we find in the *Philosophy of Right*. Show how Hegel's usage of the term, "civil society" is the result of a long philosophical tradition. Is there any new significance which Hegel gives to this term?

SAMPLE ESSAYS

1. The following theses, which Hegel discusses in his section on "civil society," offer possibilities for expansion, application, confirmation, and/or criticism: a) Education in a working society is primarily education-to-*work*; b) "law and order" results from the emergence of a distinctive "business" class in society; c) human beings are inherently *un*equal, and the notion of "human equality" is a myth; d) citizens are only responsible for obeying *promulgated* laws; e) poverty and laziness and crime are connected with the breakup of primitive family unity, which is found in civil society; and f) through the process of punishment, a man is "restored to himself."

2. Hegel, who considered America to be a "civil society" prior to statehood,* would like a wide range of powers to be invested in the public authority or "police." Which of these powers would Americans tend to consider "socialistic" in nature? Discuss the other suggested powers in the light of current liberal and/or conservative thought in the U.S.

3. For students majoring in economics: Hegel bases his analysis of "civil society" in large part on the work of 18th and 19th century political economists (Adam Smith, Ricardo, and Say). Does Hegel do justice to the economic doctrines of these men? Do you find what you would consider to be misrepresentations of any particular aspects of the theories of the political economists?

---

* See Avineri, *Hegel's Theory of the Modern State* (Cambridge: 1972), p. 43 n., p. 135.

Sub-section 3. THE STATE

The state is the concrete actuality of the idea of freedom. It is subjective freedom which has become fully objective to itself through laws and customs (immediate objectification) and through the action of individuals (mediated objectification). Or – to put it another way – it is the raw material *and* finished product of particular wills, which are willing not just particularity, but also thought-constituted universality.

The state is the emergence of a universal will among men – not just a "common will," as we have in the case of Rousseau's "social contract."* Under a "social contract," we remain in the sphere of the capricious "indeterminate" will; and the results of forming a state on such a principle were manifested dramatically in the French "Reign of Terror."

Insofar as the state is a universal will, it binds men into a divine unity (a *Volkgeist*); and thus it must be differentiated from "civil society," in which only the particular will is the end and driving force.

The Idea of the state develops itself in three moments:

A. It is embodied in the constitution and constitutional law, and takes on an individual character from this embodiment.

B. It exists as one particular state over against others.

C. It exists as *world history* – the *process* of development of, and interaction between, particular states – which rises above them and passes judgement upon them.

A. *The constitution* (§§ 260–329)

The state is the explicit unity or harmony of the universal and the particular, of the objective and the subjective, of duty and right, of necessity and freedom.

This explicit harmony was lacking in ancient states, in which insufficient

---

* Rousseau said that governments were created by a social contract, through which citizens mutually agreed to give up certain rights provided that they received other rights in exchange.

respect was given to the particular, to the subjective, i.e., to right and freedom.

In *some* modern states, however, this explicit harmony is manifest:

1) The fact that *universality* is explicitly united with *particularity* is manifest insofar as the universal organism of the state is constructed on the twofold foundation of the family and civil society (since both the family and civil society involve roles and functions which are to a great extent freely chosen, and subject to individual control). It is also manifest insofar as these modern states consider it their *duty* to promote individual *rights* and happiness (there is no split, in such a way that duties belong to the ordinary citizens, and rights belong to those in power).

2) The fact that *particularity* is explicitly united with *universality* is manifest insofar as individual interests are subordinated to family interests, or to the interests of various groupings in civil society. It is also manifest insofar as the individual finds his personal happiness in promoting the interests of his state, and jealously guards his *right* to perform his *duties* as a citizen. (Thus the dichotomy of abstract rights balanced against abstract duties disappears in the state.)

Along with the external universality and necessity of the family and of groupings in civil society, there also appears now a twofold inner universality and necessity:* a) the free assent to the duties of *patriotism* in the subjective sphere, and b) the *organic* (as opposed to organizational) *nature* of the State, in the objective sphere:

a) *Patriotism:* Patriotism is the inward sentiment which goes beyond mere opinion and subjective assurance to find certitude and *truth* for itself in the political community. The patriotic individual sees the state as the full and necessary expression of his own subjectivity. And since, in this insight, he is finding *himself* in his "other" – he is also automatically negating the otherness of that other. In other words, he does not view the state as something extrinsic to himself, but rather as his own substance.

This – and not the extraordinary fervor which is willing to make all kinds of dramatic sacrifices for one's country – is the essence of patriotism.

b) *The organic nature of the state*, which appears as the *constitution:*

The state constitution provides *content* for patriotic sentiment. It is a true organism in the political sphere, insofar as it is the universal life-substance (i.e., the thought of the people) which unfolds and diversifies itself into a stable framework of *powers* (the different agencies, channels, and functional concatenations of the state), and derives consciousness of itself in and through this process of diversification.

* Hegel is speaking here of the "universality" and "necessity" of the Idea of Reason.

A footnote on the interrelationship of Church and State:

The relationship of Church to State should be a relationship of *unity-in-distinction*. This means

1) that the Church has a *distinct* sphere of existence of its own, and should remain autonomous within that sphere. The "sphere" we are referring to here is the domain of imaginative representations of the Absolute; ritual; and those formulations of doctrine about the Absolute which give a characteristic coloring to a sect or religion (and help to differentiate it from other religions).

Since the state is the full and explicit expression of the Absolute (i.e., of the "divine" union of subjectivity and objectivity), we could say in a very limited sense that religion supplies a foundation for the state (since religion is the subjective, imaginative grasp of the Absolute – and thus can be of constructive value in educating the citizenry to a *consciousness* of the *meaning* of their political organization). But this educative function can also be fulfilled by art and philosophy.

2) that the Church, insofar as it influences the external activities of citizens, and insofar as it is itself a *corporation* – falls under the control of the state, and must remain in union with the objectives of the political order.

We are speaking here of that area of consciousness where faith gives way to understanding and rational consequences – i.e., the sphere of *knowledge*. This was formerly the sphere of the Church, in the days of barbarism which preceded modern political states. But since the Protestant reformation and the Enlightenment, it has become the peculiar province of the "secular" organism.

In other words, the Church must remain in unison with the state, and cannot be allowed to pursue a course, or assert an authority, completely of its own making.

– The order of our treatment of the state organism: First we shall consider it in its internal, constitutional aspects; secondly, we will consider it in its relationship to other state organisms:

MARX'S COMMENTARY (pp. 5–18)*

A. The Constitution

§ 261. "The state is from one point of view an external necessity [imposed on the family and civil society]."

The state takes on the aspect of an external necessity, because of the *dependence* of the family and of civil society on the constitution and laws and institutions of the particular state in which they exist.

§ 261. "On the other hand it [the state] is the end immanent within them."

This is because the duties of the individual (member of a family or civil society) to the state coalesce with his rights against the state. For example, his duty to respect property coalesces with his right to property, when we consider the relationship of "rights" to "duties" in the context of the Idea of the state.

§ 262. "The actual Idea is spirit, which sundering itself into the two spheres of its concept, family and civil society, enters upon its finite phase, but it does so only in order to rise its out of its [mere] ideality..." **

According to Hegel, the infinite and actual idea sunders itself into the two finite spheres, in order to return to itself and become "for itself."

The situation, as Hegel presents it, is one in which the state the true reality, confers rationality and existence on the two finite spheres, the family and civil society. Thus these latter become determinations of the Idea (rather than self-determinations); they are phenomena created by the absolute subject.

This is the example par excellence of the way in which Hegel makes the real into a "phenomenon," makes the exoteric esoteric, and creates out of prosaic facts a logical pantheistic mysticism:

§ 262. "The function assigned to any given individual appears to be mediated by circumstances, his caprice and his personal choice of his station in life." **

Says Marx, "the actual situation is that the assignment of the material of the state to the individual is mediated by circumstances, caprice, and personal choice of his station in life." In other words, the real subjects are the family and civil society and individual choices, and the state is the phenomenon produced *by* these subjects. But Hegel takes this exoteric situation and makes it into something esoteric. He makes it sound as if the state, the "real subject," somehow *gave rise* to a sphere of irrationality, of dark and unconscious forces where the masses of humanity work their capricious will; but continually *distinguishes itself from*, and remains outside of, this phenomenal (unreal) realm.

---

* The summary of Marx's commentary, divided in accord with Hegel's sectional headings, begins here. For the various quotations from Hegel, excerpted from Marx's commentary, the Knox translation has been used. For quotations from Marx himself, the O'Malley-Jolin translation was used. All page numbers refer to this translation.

** A slight change is made in Knox's translation here, to bring it into accord with Marx's interpretation.

§ 265. "These institutions [the social institutions and corporations which give unity and direction to the family and civil society] ... are the pillars of public freedom since in them
particular freedom is realized and rational, and therefore there is *implicitly* present even
in them the union of freedom and necessity."

§ 266. "But spirit [mind] is objective and actual to itself not merely as this necessity ..., but
also as the ideality and heart of this necessity [i.e., as an explicit *union* of freedom *and*
necessity]."

Hegel's transition here from the family and civil society to social and political institutions is not derived from the nature of the family or of civil society, but from
Spirit as the reconciliation of freedom and necessity. The reader of Hegel's *Logic*
will recall that the same rationale for transition obtains in the movement from "Essence" to "Concept", and from "Inorganic Nature" to "Life."

§ 267. "As the substance of the individual subject, [this ideal union of freedom and necessity]
is the individual's political sentiment [patriotism]; in distinction therefrom, as the
substance of the objective world, it is the organism of the state, i.e. it is the strictly
political state and its constitution."

Hegel is here distinguishing the subjective aspects of the reconciliation of freedom
and necessity (patriotism), from the objective aspect (the state "organism").

We should note that this doesn't tell us very much about how the family and civil
society fit into the state. For example, the family has already attained to existence-
for-self as *love* (see § 163 of the *Philosophy of Right*). How are we to transfer this
self-existence of the family to the pure ideality of Spirit (the state), which Hegel
makes synonymous with *knowledge* [*Wissenschaft*]?

§ 269. "The patriotic sentiment acquires its specifically determined content from the various
parts [*Seiten*] of the organism of the state. This organism is the development of the Idea
to its differences and their objective actuality ..., [i.e.] the constitution of the state."

This paragraph is an excellent example of Hegel's habit of "mystification." Hegel
starts off with the empirical observation that the state has multiple aspects, and then
goes on to say that since the state is an organism, it must diversify itself like every
organism [cf. Hegel's treatment of the "organism" in his *Logic*]. And the result of
this diversification is the development of the various aspects or powers.

In all this, he makes it seem as if he is deriving the "powers" of the state's constitution from the Idea – but in reality he is just combining one of his logical principles with a convenient empirical observation.

§ 270. "The abstract actuality or substantiality of the state consists in the fact that its end is the
universal interest..."

Hegel begins with substantiality as an abstract property or predicate of the state.

"But this substantiality of the state is its necessity, since its substantiality is divided into the
distinct spheres...."

Here the abstract substantiality becomes related to its necessary determination, i.e.
becomes actualized.

"But this very substantiality of the state is spirit (mind) knowing and willing itself after passing
through the forming process of education."

Here we should note that "substantiality," which started out as an abstract property
of spirit (the subject), is now presented as the concrete subject in which everything

else becomes a property (including spirit and all the powers or functions of spirit).

In other words, spirit becomes a predicate of its own predicate! The abstract becomes the concrete.

Conversely, what happens to the real concrete determinations – i.e. the universal interest, the various "powers," the educated spirit? They become abstract determinations produced by the logical entity, "substantiality."

This Hegelian analysis would be more appropriate to his *Logic* than the *Philosophy of Right*.

1). The inner constitution of the state, in its existence-for-self* (§§ 272–274)

Before examining the state constitution in detail, we should make a few prefatory remarks:

a) the constitution cannot be adequately comprehended by the abstract understanding, which sees the state as a sort of common denominator resulting from the balancing of one independent power against another; this is where Kant, Fichte, and others went astray in their consideration of the state;

b) neither can it be comprehended by intuition and sentiment, as von Heller and the Romantics would have us believe;

c) neither can it be imposed without taking into account the factual situation of a people, as Napoleon tried to do with the Spanish; but rather, it must develop in accord with the specific characteristics of a national personality;

d) neither can it be analyzed in terms of the *number* of people in power (this is the basis for the outmoded division of forms of government into "monarchical" (one man ruling), aristocratic (a few men ruling), and democratic (the majority ruling)). Such divisions were appropriate only to a time in history before governments became highly complexified;

e) the tripartite division of powers into legislative, executive, and *judicial* is defective, insofar as the *judiciary* is not the moment of "individuality" (i.e., it does not synthesize the universal enactments of the legislative, with the particular applications of the executive);**

f) finally, when we speak of "monarch" in regard to the constitution, we definitely do not have in mind Montesquieu's "monarchy of honor" – which is a feudal type of monarchy based on privilege, before the synthesis of duty and right had been attained.

– With these things in mind, we may now go on to observe that, if we analyze constitutional government in accord with the concept of Reason (the dialectical unity of opposites), we find that it develops itself by means of three major and essential powers –

a) *the legislative* (representing universality)

b) *the executive* (concerned with applications to particularity)

c) *the Crown* (in which particularity is synthesized *with* universality into *individuality* with the right of ultimate decision-making)

Note: since the constitution of the state is an organism, it permeates each of the different "powers" equally; however, in doing so it emphasizes different aspects differently: and this results in the differentiation of the powers.

---

* See glossary.

** This observation (e) comes from the Addenda, following Hegel's *Philosophy of Right*. For Hegel's meaning of "Individual," see Glossary. p. 10

MARX'S COMMENTARY (pp. 19–20)

1. The inner constitution of the state, in its existence-for-self

§ 272. "The constitution is rational in so far as the state inwardly differentiates and determines its activity in accordance with the nature of the concept. The result of this is that each of [the powers that develop from the concept] is in itself the totality of the constitution . . . '

Once again this shows how in Hegel the Concept is not conformed to the state, but rather the State must conform to the Concept.

§ 273. "The state as a political entity is thus cleft into three substantitive divisions [a) the legislature; b) the executive; and c) the Crown]."

[After "thus," Marx writes ("how 'thus'?"). He indicates that he will return to this division later (starting with § 275).]

§ 274. ". . . The Constitution of any given nation depends in general on the character and development of its self-consciousness."

All Hegel is saying here is that the constitution should faithfully reflect the particular stage of self-consciousness which has been reached by a nation. If he would follow out his own principle to its conclusion, he would have to say that man should be the principle of the constitution. But he doesn't say this.

(a) The crown (§§ 275–286)

In St. Anselm's Ontological proof for the existence of God, we have the unity of the Concept with Existence – by means of a particular concept which is not just a concept, but must necessarily exist.*

So also, in the monarch, we have the unity of the concept of state sovereignty with existence – by means of a particular branch of state power which is not just delegated to a person by the "people," but belongs to a particular individual as a birthright (i.e., just because he *exists*).

In order to understand this, we should take the following facts into consideration:

(1) Sovereignty as an attribute of the state is a purely ideal unity, and is distributed to this or that particular functionary of the state in much the same way that the power of the soul is distributed to the many faculties of a man – i.e., as something simultaneously given and taken away;

(2) If the sovereignty of the persons or subjects of a nation is to come into *existence* at all, it must come into existence as a particular subjectivity, a particular personality – namely the existent Sovereign, who possesses, within limits fixed by the constitution, the ultimate decision-making power, the ultimate veto-power.

Nations which lack such a sovereign will lack stability and sovereignty itself, since the freedom of personal decision-making in such nations will always be something *conditioned* by artificial "persons" – i.e, by committees, etc. But it is necessary that freedom in the state, like freedom in the individual should manifest its completely *unconditioned* character.

The necessity of some particular embodiment of unconditioned ("divine") authority becomes especially evident in times of internal and external crisis and turmoil, when swift and firm decisions are necessary.

Nations like Britain, which lose or no longer have a sovereign in the strict sense, *ipso facto* lose their sovereignty in the strict sense.

(3) The sovereignty which is invested in a particular individual must belong to him through *nature*, i.e., by birth. There are some good reasons for this:

In states which are lacking in full organic development, the assignation of sovereign power takes place through external, conditioning factors – through fate, or civil or military crises. For example, in ancient Greece, people would derive the last word on conducting governmental affairs from an oracle,

---

* St. Anselm said that with every concept, except the concept of God, you can ask the question, "does it exist." You can't do this with the concept of God. however, because it is impossible to think of God as *not* existing. Thus the concept of God shows a "unity" with existence.

or from divination; and in our own times military leaders and "men of destiny" are often brought into political sovereignty by crises and emergencies.

It is necessary, however, that in a fully developed, rational state, the emergence of sovereign power should be set beyond such external conditioning factors – i.e., should be unconditioned, like personality itself. And the only way to do this is through a ruling family. (This suggestion, of course, will be distasteful to those advocates of analytic Understanding, who have never grasped the concrete unity of mind and nature – and who seem to believe that the ultimate decision-making power could reside in something other than a concrete, natural person).

If we consider the Crown according to its "aspects," the following analysis results:

1) It is the *unity* of universality and particularity. This implies a) that the monarchy should exhibit the unity of unconditioned universal selfhood (absolute decision-making power) and unconditioned particular existence (natural, hereditary succession to the throne) – a unity which puts monarchy beyond all the caprices and contingencies of an "elected" monarchy. It implies b) that the monarch should have the power to apply the more universal categories (e.g., religion) to particular spheres (e.g., right and wrong) – and thus the monarch has the power to pardon criminals.

2) The monarchy also manifests control over the *particular*, especially in its relationship to the supreme council, whose task it is to gather all relevant objective data on affairs of state, in order to assist the monarch in making the final decision.

3) It manifests *universality* especially as regards the subjective conscience of the monarch, in his relationship to the universal constitutional laws of his nation.

MARX'S COMMENTARY (pp. 20–40)

(a) The crown

> § 275. "The power of the crown contains in itself the three moments of the whole: α) the *universality* of the constitution and the laws; β) counsel, which refers the *particular* to the universal; and γ) the moment of ultimate decision, as the *self-determination* to which everything else reverts and from which everything else derives the beginning of actuality."

In his reference to "universality" here, Hegel makes it seem as if the monarch were subject to the [universal] laws and the constitution. But the real power of the monarch becomes revealed in the reference to *self-determination*. Hegel goes on to say (in the same paragraph) that the "*absolute self-determination* of the monarch constitutes the distinctive principle of the power of the crown." In an ordinary individual, such power of self-determination is called an "actual" will (cf. § 12 of the *Philosophy of Right*). But in the case of the monarch, insofar as the monarch can absolutely divorce himself from the constitution and laws (which an individual cannot do) – this power of "self-determination" is only an abstract, rather superficial self-determination – what Hegel calls "arbitrariness" (*Willkür* – § 15).

> § 276. "[The authority of particular powers and activities in the state] is no independent authority, but only an authority of an order and breadth determined by the *Idea of the whole; from its might* they originate...."

Hegel subsumes the authority of the various "powers and activities" under the rationality of the Idea of the state. But *insofar* as these powers and activities are considered as the external necessity of multifarious contingencies – they could *not* be subsumed into the rationality of the state. Hegel doesn't take this fact into consideration.

> § 277. "The individual functionaries and agents [of the state] are attached to their office not on the strength of their immediate personality, but only on the strength of their universal and objective qualities. Hence it is in an external and contingent way that these offices are linked with particular persons...."

Hegel speaks here as if the activities of the state were related in only a "contingent" way to individual personalities. This is absurd. The functions of the state are *necessarily* related to individual persons, because of the essentially *social* nature of individual human beings.

> § 278, *Remark* "... In times of peace, the particular spheres and functions pursue the path o satisfying their particular aims and minding their own business, and it is in part only by way of the unconscious necessity of the thing that their self-seeking is turned into a contribution to reciprocal support and to the support of the whole.... In part, however,it is by direct influence of higher authority that they are not only continually brought back to the aims of the whole and restricted accordingly ..., but are also constrained to perform direct services for the support of the whole.
> "In a situation of exigency, however, whether in home or foreign affairs, the organism of which these particular spheres are members fuses into the single concept of sovereignty.... It is then that ideality comes into its proper actuality."

During peacetime, the particular powers and functions of the state are so involved in the "war" or exigency of self-seeking that their ideal unity with the state sovereignty is never actually and explicitly achieved. But during a situation of war or exigency the private wars and exigencies of the state's functionaries become explicitly manifested [projected onto some external nation] – and thus the unity of these functionaries with the sovereignty of their state becomes actualized!

§ 279. "Sovereignty, at first the universal *thought* of [the ideality of the state], comes into *existence* only as subjectivity sure of itself."

If we were to take these words at their face value, they would indicate that sovereignty as essence or substance can only become existent in and through the persons or subjects which make up a society (since no single person could exhaust all the content of sovereignty).

But then Hegel goes on to say:

"Sovereignty ... comes into existence only ... as the will's abstract and to that extent ungrounded self-determination.... This absolutely decisive moment of the whole is not individuality in general, but a single individual, the monarch."

The state as a unified natural entity has individuality, i.e. it is an individual state. But the sovereignty of the state is not sufficiently expressed in *that* individual. It must be expressed not only as a natural entity, but as a person. And the monarch, according to Hegel, supplies the means for this expression. Why the monarch? Hegel goes on to explain,

"Each of the three moments of the concept has its explicitly actual and separate formation."

In other words, since "*unity*" (of particularity and universality) is one of the moments of the Concept (along with "*particularity*" and "*universality*"), this moment of unity should be entitled to an explicit and separate formation, i.e. in the monarch. But why couldn't the unity of universal law and particular decision-making power be found in the individual *citizen* of the state?

Or we might also ask: what about the other "moments" Shouldn't *they* be entitled to an "explicitly actual and separate formation"? For example, the "universal moment, legislation. Shouldn't this be incarnated in a single individual by the same line of reasoning?

But all this is simply another example of Hegel's habit of mystification: First of all, he takes the common-sense observation that sovereignty is a predicate of the people, and makes it seem as if the people were a predicate of sovereignty, which has become the subject. Then, in order to give philosophical formation to the empirical fact that the monarch *has* the last word (sovereignty), he says the monarch *is* the last word (the ultimate expression of sovereignty). Let us go on to some of Hegel's remarks on the same paragraph:

§ 279, *Remarks* "Hence it is the basic moment of personality, abstract at the start in immediate rights, which has matured itself through its various forms of subjectivity, and now ... has become the personality of the state."

According to Hegel, the monarch manifests the *concrete* epitome of personality, which begins its development at the "immediate" stage of abstract right (see § 34 of the *Philosophy of Right*). But in reality, the monarch, as personified sovereignty, becomes an *abstract* (exclusive) form of sovereignty.*

* See next page.

"Personality, like subjectivity in general, as infinitely self-related, has its truth ... only in a person."

Hegel reasons that, because subjectivity is actual only as subject, and the subject actual only as one (i.e. some single person), *therefore the personality of the state is actual only as one person.* He could just as well conclude that, because the individual man is one (a single person), therefore the essence of individual men is one single person.

"A so-called 'artificial person,' be it a society, a community, or a family ... contains personality only abstractly. In an 'artificial person,' personality has not yet achieved its true mode of existence. The state, however, is precisely this totality in which the moments of the concept have attained actuality...."

Instead of recognizing that persons attain their actuality in and through such species-forms as the family, a particular community, etc. – Hegel makes it seem as if all actuality of personality developed out of the abstract concept of the state.

"To be something not deduced [by the demonstrations of political philosophers of *raisonnement*] but purely self-originating is precisely the concept of monarchy."

[In response to this, Marx writes: "In a certain sense every inevitable existent is purely self-originating, in this respect the monarch's louse as well as the monarch."]

"We may speak of the 'sovereignty of the people' in the sense that any people whatever is self-subsistent vis-a-vis other peoples, and constitutes a state of its own."

It is rather out of character for Hegel to make such a concession. He has already limited all *actual* sovereignty to the sole person of the monarch. The monarch can represent the sovereignty of the state quite well by himself – even without the people.

"Taken without its monarch and the articulation of the whole which is the indispensable and direct concomitant of the monarchy, the people is a formless mass and no longer a state."

This is, of course, only true in Hegel's system: because Monarchy, by his definition, is that which gives form and meaning to the people.

"If by 'sovereignty of the people' is understood a republican form of government, or to speak more specifically ... a democratic form, then ... such a notion cannot be further discussed in face of the Idea of the state in its full development."

According to Hegel, Monarchy, as the highest development of the Idea, is the standard by which democracy can be judged. Monarchy is the "truth" of democracy, the explicit development of trends and aspirations that are only incomplete in democracy. But just the opposite is the case. Democracy is the truth of monarchy.

In ancient forms of government – even in Greece – the private life of citizens was subsumed into the nation or the *res publica*. There was no real private life and existence. In the Middle Ages, there was a semblance of freedom and private life, because political structures became more closely identified with private interests. But this was the democracy of non-freedom. In order for real democracy to arrive, it was first necessary that free commerce and possession of property (the private spheres) should attain an autonomy of their own. Then the way is prepared for de-

* "The monarch is personified sovereignty, sovereignty become man, incarnate state-consciousness, whereby all other persons are thus excluded from this sovereignty, from personality, and from state-consciousness." – Marx, *Critique*, O'Malley ed., p. 26.

mocracy in several stages: a) the political state begins to appear as the form which restricts and determines the "content" of the "private sphere", the politico-social nature of men existing extrinsic to, and alienated from, men; b) the monarch becomes (in the modern world) the fullest expression of man's alienation of his political essence from himself; c) the "republic" (and also, to a certain extent, the "constitutional monarchy" appears as the negation of this alienation, but still existing alongside the alienation (the abstract form of state sovereignty); d) democracy brings with it the abolition of this abstract state-form, with the result that the distinction between form and content disappears; the people determine the constitution instead of being determinations of the constitution*; the whole is no longer determined by the part; and the essence of man (as a *social* being) appears finally as a specific "form of government" (just as in Christianity the essence of all religion (the deification of man) appeared as a particular form of religion).

§ *280*. "This ultimate self ... is, when thus taken in abstraction, a single self and therefore is immediate individuality. Hence its natural character is implied in its very conception.... *This* individual is raised to the dignity of monarch in an immediate, natural fashion, i.e. *through his birth* in the course of nature.... The transition ... *is the immediate conversion of the pure self-determination of the will ... into a single and natural existent* without the mediation of a particular content (like a purpose in the case of action)."

Hegel bases himself on an empirical fact that subjective wills are corporeal individuals who come into existence by birth. But he goes on to make an "immediate" speculative connection between natural birth and sovereignty of will. This connection is *so* immediate and unprecedented that it is a good example of the art of magic operating in the name of philosophical speculation, to unify contradictions in an irrational way. "Hegel has demonstrated that the monarch must be born, which no one questions, but not that birth makes one a monarch" (*Critique*, p. 33). If we take him literally, however, he is saying that abstract natural determinacy would determine the quality of the monarch, just as it determines the quality of cattle. However, Hegel is wrong when he says there is no medium – e.g. some mediating purpose – to explain this transition from nature to will. "The medium here is the absolute will and the word of the philosopher; the particular end is the end of the philosophizing subject, namely constructing the hereditary monarch out of the pure Idea; and the actualization of the end is Hegel's simple affirmation."

§ *281*. "Both moments in their undivided unity – (a) the will's ultimate ungrounded self, and (b) therefore its similarly ungrounded objective existence (existence being the category which is at home in nature) – constitute the Idea of something against which caprice is powerless."

The two moments which are unified in the monarch are (a) the contingency of the capricious will; and (b) the contingency of nature (i.e., birth). And this collision of two contingencies is supposed to be a safeguard against all contingencies!

§ *282*. "The right to pardon criminals arises from the sovereignty of the monarch, since it is this alone which is empowered to actualize spirit's power of making undone what has been done and wiping out a crime by forgiving and forgetting it."

* "In all states distinct from democracy the state, the law, the constitution is dominant without really governing, that is, materially permeating the content of the remaining non-political spheres. In democracy the constitution, the law, the state, so far as it is political constitution, is itself only a self-determination of the people, and a determinate content of the people." (Marx, *Critique*, p. 31).

The pardoning of criminals is the ultimate expression of capriciousness or arbitrary will. It is significant that Hegel makes this the primary prerogative of the monarch (who is himself the embodiment of caprice).

§ 283, 284. "When [the moment of particularity] acquires a special objective existence, it becomes the supreme council. ... The individuals who discharge these duties are in direct contact with the person of the monarch and therefore the choice and dismissal alike of these individuals rest with his unrestricted caprice.

"It is only for the *objective* side of decision, i.e., for knowledge of the problem and the attendant circumstances, and for the legal and other reasons which determine its solution, that men are answerable. ... The personal majesty of the monarch, on the other hand, as the final *subjectivity* of decision, is above all answerability for acts of government."

Here Hegel takes an empirical fact – the immunity of the monarch from responsibility in government – and tries to justify it philosophically. All the responsibility for checking the objective facts, etc. – is left to the council (the "objective" aspect of the monarch's will). The monarch himself, as the "final subjectivity" bears no responsibility for the decision he makes [and in fact does not even have the responsibility to consult with his council, or to make sure of the council's "objectivity."]

§ 285. "The third moment in the power of the crown concerns the absolute universality which subsists subjectively in the conscience of the monarch and objectively in the whole of the constitution and the laws."

In a constitutional monarchy such as Hegel depicts, the constitution certainly does *not* insure the objectivity of the *monarch*, but guarantees to him the right of being subjectively irresponsible.

"Hence the power of the crown presupposes the other moments in the state just as it is presupposed by them."

This *should* imply that the choice and power of the monarch is established not by birth, but by the other moments, i.e. the council and the laws. But, of course, this is not Hegel's meaning.

§ 286. "In the rational organism of the state, each member, by maintaining itself in its own position, *eo ipso* maintains the others in theirs."

This would seem to imply that none of these inter-dependent moments could be fixed and unalterable. But it doesn't.

Résumé of Remarks to § 279:
"The peoples of England, Scotland . . . etc. are not sovereign peoples at all, now that they have ceased to have rulers or supreme governments of their own."

Hegel shows here that the basis for the sovereignty of the monarch is nationality [or nationalism?], and the cleft between nationalities is expressed in the cleft between these "absolute" individuals.

"In an 'artificial person,' personality has not achieved its true mode of existence. The state, however, is precisely this totality in which the moments of the concept have attained the actuality correspondent to their degree of truth."

According to Hegel, "artificial persons," including the state, have personality in only an abstract way; and this personality must be concretized in a single empirical individual – the monarch. Thus two very simple things – birth (of the monarch) and private property (the primogeniture operative in the royal family) – become the terminus of a very complex process. And what is it that distinguishes the monarch from all others? His natural existence, his body. And what is the highest function of the body? Sexual activity. Therefore the highest function of the monarch is to create other monarchs through sexual activity.

Amidst all this mystification, there is one lesson that we should not miss: When Hegel says that the monarch is the abstract person who has the state in him, he is recognizing in an upside-down way that the essence of the state *is* the abstract private person. In other words, the secret about the monarch is that "he is the lone private person in whom the relation of the private person *in general* to the state is actualized." (p. 40).

(b) The executive (§§ 287–297)

The executive branch is concerned with implementing the constitution and the decision of the monarch – i.e., with applying the "universal" to particular cases. It is composed of civil servants and advisory officials, who are organized into various spheres of activity or into committees, under a supreme civil servant (e.g., a prime minister) and a supreme advisory official or spokesman. However, just as the executive power converges at the top, it should also converge at the bottom – e.g., in the mayor, whose job it is to apply the directives of the post office executives, the public Health executives, etc.

Executives in government should be chosen exclusively on the basis of ability and skill – in such a way that executive positions are open to all classes of the general populace (although the fitting of man-to-job depends ultimately on the subjective will of the monarch). They should be paid sufficiently, so that there will be no temptation to bribery or misuse of public funds. They should have tasks which are well-defined (although the essential "task" of the executive is spiritual in nature, and cannot be judged purely on the basis of objective results).

In relationship to the Corporations (commercial, professional, and municipal corporations), the task of the executive is to keep in contact with this sphere of particularity, to balance private vs. common interests, and to balance all interests against the requirements of the state – without infringing on the jurisdiction of the corporations (which includes the power to nominate officials, subject to the approval of the executive branch).

All in all, the class of executives constitutes a "middle-class" in the best sense. It is generally superior not only in skills and techniques, but in ethical sentiment and refinement. It is essentially characterized by conscience, politeness, a dispassionate treatment of all, and a freedom from private self-seeking for oneself and one's family and friends (this latter characteristic is found more consistently and naturally in larger states, where family ties, etc. are less prominent). Nevertheless, a public executive may misuse his freedom in a purely capricious way; and in such cases his action often takes on the character, not just of inefficiency or negligence, but of a *crime* against the state.

MARX'S COMMENTARY (pp. 41–54)

(b) The executive

"There is a distinction between the monarch's decisions and their execution.... This task of ... subsuming the particular under the universal is comprised in the executive power, which also includes the powers of the judiciary and the police."

Hegel delegates to the executive power the task of executing in particular ways the "universal" decisions of the monarch. There is nothing too original about this, except that Hegel includes the judiciary along with the executive power – whereas the judiciary is usually considered to be opposed to the executive.

§ 288. "Particular interests which are common to everyone fall within civil society.... The administration of these is in the hands of corporations.... These circles of particular interest must be subordinated to the higher interest of the state."

[Marx comments: "This is a simple description of the empirical situation in some countries." – p. 41].

§ 289. "Civil society is the battlefield where everyone's individual interest meets everyone else's.... The corporation mind, engendered when the particular spheres gain their title to rights, is now inwardly converted into the mind of the state.... This is the secret of the patriotism of the citizens.... In the corporation mind the rooting of the particular in the universal is directly entailed."

Thus we see that the secret of patriotism is the convergence of the private egotistical interests of the "burghers" of civil society into common aims.

Why does not Hegel oppose the *family* man, as well as the "burgher," to the state? Since it is the essence of the absolute will to develop itself in these three directions, one would expect something like this. But Hegel seems to consider family – for some strange reason – as more in line with the "absolute will" than civil society.

§ 290. [The division of labor in the executive power fans out into various abstract branches, and then converges again in concrete areas of civil life.]

§ 291. [Appointment as a "civil servant" (*dem allgemeinen Stande*) is dependent solely on knowledge and proof of ability.]

§ 292. "The linking of two things, a man and his office, which in relation to each other must always be fortuitous, is the *subjective* aspect of election to office, and it must lie with the crown...."

§ 293. [The powers and functions of public officials constitute one part of the sovereignty of the crown.]

§ 294. [The executive should have his particular needs satisfied, to make sure that he will not pursue his own private interest or profit in serving the state.... He must fulfil his duties faithfully or be subject to dismissal.]

§ 295. [There are two natural "checks" to the potential irresponsibility of public officials: the hierarchical state control from above; and the authority of societies and Corporations from below.]

§ 296. [Two factors – a) ethical education, and b) the size and complexity of the state organism –help to produce a "dispassionate, upright, and polite demeanor" in civil servants, without narrow provincialism.]

§ 297. "Civil servants and the members of the executive constitute the greater part of the middle class....* The sovereign working on the middle class at the top, and the Corporation-

* Hegel is not using the term, "middle class" in the socio-economic sense in which it is currently used. His "middle class" is the political middle class – those who dispense power from above to below.

rights working on it at the bottom ... effectively prevent it from acquiring the isolated position of an aristocracy."

Hegel's description is partly an empirical description of the way the bureaucracy is, and partly an empirical description of the way it thinks it is.

Hegel does not develop the content of the bureaucracy, since the bureaucracy is the [content-less] formalism of the corporation.

Hegel makes it appear as if the bureaucracy and the corporation were engaged in a kind of constructive opposition. But if civil society ever threatens to destroy the corporation, the opposition of the bureaucracy to the corporation will immediately cease, since the bureaucracy is the "Corporation" (independent group interest) of the state, just as the corporation is the bureaucracy of civil society. In this regard, "the bureaucracy must defend the imaginary universality of particular interest, i.e. the "corporation mind," in order to defend the imaginary particularity of the universal interests, i.e. its own mind." Thus the bureaucracy and the corporation have an identity of interests, in spite of their conflict.

Insofar as the bureaucracy is the formalism of the state (the Jesuitical tissue of spiritual illusion), it tries to erect this essence of formalism into the goal of the state. In other words, the bureaucracy itself becomes the goal of the state. And insofar as this formalism is its *secret* essence, it strives to avoid making the bureaucratic mind and processes public. It is committed to secrecy. And as a paradoxical result, this pure spiritualism or formalism, ossified in perpetuating its own state's traditions and dehumanized machinery, becomes a crass materialism, an unwitting reflection of its own conception of real life as something crass and material outside the bureaucracy.

Just as the Catholic Church is the real existence of the sovereignty of the "Blessed Trinity," so also the bureaucracy is the real existence of the identity of universal interest and private aim which is supposed to exist in the state. But, of course, the bureaucracy is identified with the "particular" interests of the people only as an abstraction; it is really concerned only with promoting the particular interest of the bureaucracy. In view of this, we may conjecture that "the abolition [Aufhebung] of the bureaucracy can consist only in the universal interest becoming really – and not, as with Hegel, becoming purely in thought, in abstraction – a particular interest; and this is possible only through the particular interest [of the people] really becoming universal" (p. 48).

In Hegel's formulation, then, the identity of the executive with particular interests is quite the opposite of a true dialectic identity-in-distinction; it is a *mixtum compositum*, resulting from the mixed choice (or compromise) by which the higher authorities and the corporations and societies get together to nominate intermediate executives.

§ 289. "The maintenance of the state's universal interest, and of legality, in this sphere of particular right, and the work of bringing these rights back to the universal, require to be superintended by holders of the executive power...."

In the domain of the state, the executive office holders are the true representatives – not "of" – but "against" civil society. They are set up in fixed opposition to civil society.

§ 291. "The nature of the executive functions is that they are objective and ... have been explicitly fixed by previous decisions."

This is a reference to the decisions of the crown, which prevent the emergence of any "natural" link between an individual and the executive functions which are assigned to him.

§ *291.* "The objective factor in their appointment is knowledge and proof of ability...."

Just as every Catholic layman has a chance to become a priest, every member of civil society could (by passing an examination) become a member of the "Universal Class." In each case, he who enters the "higher" class is a deserter, becoming a member of the other hostile army. The "examination" of the potential executive is not concerned with essential state knowledge (requisite for being a good citizen), but with the initiation requirements for the Masonic rites, through which the "profane" knowledge of the former "burgher" becomes the holy knowledge of the privileged executive.

§ *292.* "The linking of two things, a man and his office, which in relation to each other must always be fortuitous, is the subjective aspect of election to office, and it must lie with the crown...."

Here again the prince becomes the representative of chance and contingency (arbitrary will). He delegates functions to whomever he wills (and brings about a "rational" identity of the state and civil society through the mediating force which he possesses – the salary of the civil servants).

§ *294, Remarks* "What the service of the state ... requires is that men shall forgo the selfish and capricious satisfaction of their subjective ends...."

This is true of every servant. The special stability of civil servants is due to the salary which guarantees their existence. The "honesty" of civil servants is due a) to the hierarchical organization against which the civil servant cannot sin, but which exonerates him from the sins he commits for its sake; and b) the unresolved conflict between the bureaucracy and the corporation – which keeps the civil servant from usurping privileges from civil society.

In § 296, Hegel goes on to say that the "dispassionate, upright, and polite demeanor" of civil servants is 1) partly a result of ethical education which acts as a mental counterpoise to his mechanical activity, and 2) partly a result of the size of the state. But in regard to 1), it would be truer to say that his mechanical activity is the effective counterpoise to his ethical conduct, and in regard to 2), we could simply point to the example of Russia, where the great size of the country gives no guarantee against the caprice of civil servants.

In § 297, Hegel states that maintaining an "organic unity" is possible "only by giving authority to spheres of particular interests, which are relatively independent, and by appointing an army of officials whose personal arbitrariness is broken against such authorized bodies." Thus we find that, by some miracle, an organic unity is produced by the counterbalancing of privileges.

(c) The legislature (§§ 298–320)

Since a legislature is an *essential part* of the organic totum of the state constitution, it would not be quite correct to say that it is "determined by"
the constitution – although it is obvious that changes in the constitution will
have reciprocal effects on the legislature.

The legislative branch, as the organ of government especially concerned
with the aspect of *universality* in the state, has two primary functions: 1)
to protect the interest of the citizens; and 2) to demand services from them.
The first function is fulfilled by the process of making determinate laws (i.e.,
neither too general, nor too particular) in regard to the welfare of the various
corporations, organizations and private individuals in the state. The second
function (in modern states, which recognize the right of free subjectivity to
determine one's own labor, etc.) is fulfilled through taxation – which, by
means of the universalizing medium of *money*, reduces *direct* control over
the activities of citizens.

The members of the legislature are influenced in their deliberations from
three legitimate sources: 1) from the crown; 2) from the executive branch
(which has special knowledge and experience of facts and circumstances)
relevant to proposed legislation; and 3) from the two Houses of the Estates*
– who represent the two main interests of civil society – the agricultural interests and the business interests.

The Estates do not, of course, have any special insight into their own needs.
They do, however have special insight into the administration of the particular public officials who are dealing with their members; and for this reason, they have something important to offer for the deliberations of the legislature. Likewise, the formation of the *"hoi polloi"* of civil society into the
organized form of the Estates, offers the following additional advantages: a)
it keeps the various executive officials "on their toes," to avoid the criticism
or wrath of the public; b) it prevents the formation of an unorganized mob
or rabble, whose only solution, in a constitutional government, would be to
overthrow the constitution by force; c) it reduces the dangers of opposition,
since the very act of organizing into Estates is a sign of essential cooperation
with the Constitution; d) it gives the legislature access to the "empirical
universal," i.e., the general circumstances of the masses, as mediated and
interpreted with the help of the executive branch of government.

The Two Houses of the Estates:

1) *The Upper House* consists of the landed gentry, who exhibit a notable resemb-

---

* A parliamentary body in Hegel's time. It should be noted that the Estates are only a
part of the "Legislature," along with the Crown and members of the Executive branch.

lance to the monarchy, insofar as they are self-subsistent (not subject to business concerns, etc.), and receive their position through inheritance (which is protected through the laws of primogeniture), rather than through election.

The members of this class have the privilege of presenting themselves in person at sessions of the Estates; and they act as a mediation between the free subjectivity of the Crown, and the free subjectivities represented by the lower house. Often they prevent the lower house from becoming an irrational block of public opinion; but sometimes, in siding with the lower house, they prevent the lower house from being denounced by the Crown for irrationality or whimsy.

2) *The Lower House* consists of deputies from civil society (the various corporations, etc.). These deputies do not have an open invitation to be present at the deliberations of the Crown, but must receive a summons. Ideally, they should be elected from the *ranks* of the specific Corporations concerned (since election in a rational society must be representative in form, if it is to be effective at all.) But those who are elected should have given solid evidence not only of experience and proficiency in the business of their corporation, but also of acumen and trustworthiness in matters of public concern.

– *The Two Houses of the Estates* are not an absolute necessity for the operation of government, but they do give added efficiency to government insofar as they keep the members of government in contact with the formal freedom of civil society (which does justice to the principle of "subjectivity," which has gained preeminence in modern states). Also, it exerts a definite educative influence upon the populace at large, keeps them informed as to what are the substantial issues, and keeps them from becoming a mass of uneducated opinions.

– *Public opinion* is characteristically a mixture of valid public concerns with merely private interests. Only the leader who knows how to ignore the accidental caprices of public opinion, while espousing and promoting its valid concerns, can be truly great.

Censorship of speech and of newspapers becomes a necessity if and when subjective freedom gets to the point of advocating the overthrow of the free state. Since the free state is the *guarantee* of subjective freedom – its "free" overthrow would be a self-contradiction.

It is very hard to decide on questions of censorship, however, since the emotional enuciations of public opinion are very often indeterminate and subjective, and offer offense only in a very subtle manner (i.e., they do not openly attack, by word or deed, the person of the monarch or other agencies of government). In such cases it should be kept in mind that such excesses are very often just the result of festering resentment which looks for an outlet. Such resentment either carries with it no real threat, or else is cancelled out by the scorn of contrary elements of public opinion.

MARX'S COMMENTARY (pp. 54–127)

(c) The legislature

§ 298. "The legislature is itself a part of the constitution which is presupposed by it and to that extent lies absolutely outside the sphere directly determined by it; nonetheless, the constitution becomes progressively more mature in the course of the further elaboration of the laws...."

Hegel, as usual, begins with the opposite of the way things really are. He tries to make it seem as if the legislature developed out of the constitution. This is true of the legislature as a constitutional power (*assemblée constituée*), but not of the legislature as the power of the constitution (*assemblée constituante*). The legislature in the latter sense must, of course, preceed the constitution.

"Directly," Hegel says, the constitution lies absolutely outside the sphere of the legislature. But "nonetheless," the constitution becomes "more mature." This is because the legislature modifies the constitution "indirectly." In fact, the legislature picks the constitution apart piece-by-piece until it contradicts the letter and spirit of the original – and Hegel does not resolve the antinomy between what the legislature should be (the defender of the constitution) and what it is (the transformer of the constitution).

§ 298, Addition "The constitution must in and by itself be the fixed and recognized ground on which the legislature stands, and for this reason it must not first be constructed."

The appearance here contradicts the reality. The appearance is that the constitution remains as the ultimate guarantee of the freedom of self-conscious reason in the state. The reality is that by a kind of "natural necessity" the constitution becomes altered, to the detriment of the freedom of consciousness (in the manner that all state property in the German state was transformed "constitutionally" into the private property of the German princes and their families).

In order to produce a completely new constitution, however, revolutions have always been necessary.

§ 298, Additions (cont.) "The advance from one state of affairs to another ... is tranquil in appearance and unnoticed."

This is simply false. It would be true if the progress of the people were made the cornerstone of the constitution, and written into the constitution. But *de facto* the major constitutional changes in favor of the people until the present have come about through the legislative (the representative of the people), which has produced great organic, universal revolutions by attacking antiquated constitutions. (The revolutions produced by the executive have been, in contrast, reactive movements not to establish a new constitution, but to supercede the "obstacles" which the constitution placed in their way.)

Of course it should be recognized that the problems Hegel has to deal with are precisely problems resulting from the unnatural split of the state into the formalistic "political" state and the "non-political" state (the people). Once the people repossess their natural right to give *themselves* their constitution, questions about "whether the legislative determines the constitution or vice versa" will become superfluous. In such a case, the legislature will not make the law, but merely discover and formulate the laws that exist among the people. But until that time, the legislature will continue to function in a rather ambivalent fashion in connection with the constitution [of republics and constitutional monarchies], which is simply a compromise between the political and non-political state.

§ 299. "Legislative business is more precisely determined in relation to private individuals, under these two heads: (a) provision by the state for their well being and happiness, and (b) the exaction of services from them.... As for the services to be exacted, it is only if these are reduced to terms of money ... that they can be fixed justly...."

Hegel's reasoning is that, in order to avoid demanding specific services from citizens (a demand which would infringe on "subjective freedom"), the modern state resorts to taxation, etc. – by means of which the individual, while contributing to the state, is left free to decide how he will acquire or earn his contribution. Hegel's motto here is "do what you want, pay what you must! (p. 60)"

The only exception Hegel makes to this rule is military service. We shall consider this exception later.

§ 299. Remark "The proper object of universal legislation may be distinguished in a general way from the proper function of administrative officials or of some kind of state regulation, in that the content of the former [i.e. of universal legislation] is wholly universal, i.e. determinate laws, while it is what is particular in content which falls to the latter.... The organic unity of the powers of the state itself implies that it is one single mind which both firmly established the universal and also brings it into its determinate actuality and carries it out."

If Hegel had really succeeded in constructing such an "organic unity" – this passage would make sense. But as it is, he shows no real unity between legislature (the universal) and executive (the particular). De facto they are in collision, just as the leggislature and the constitution are in collision.

§ 300. "In the legislature as a whole the other powers are the first two moments which are effective, (i) the monarchy as that to which ultimate decisions belong; (ii) the executive as the advisory body.... The last moment in the legislature is the Estates."*

We can see from this that the third and last moment (the Estates) are from one point of view a part of the legislature (in the sense that the "legislature" includes everything); but from another point of view constitutes the "mere legislature" (in distinction from the monarchy and the executive).

§ 301. "The Estates have the function of bringing public affairs into existence not only implicitly, but also actually, i.e., of bringing into existence the moment of subjective formal freedom, the public consciousness as an empirical universal...."

Since Hegel has already given to the bureaucracy an essence which is foreign to it (the public consciousness), it is not surprising that he grants to the real public consciousness only the status of the inferior form of an appearance – the "empirical universal." And since the true content of freedom in-itself has already been mystically established in the bureaucracy (the subject), the estates (as the predicate)

* "Within the legislative body of the Estates representatives of the various civil and political elements – the crown, the bureaucracy, and the civil estates – meet to debate and determine the course of the nation-state." – O'Malley, Introduction to Marx's Critique, p. L.

become the pure formality or illusion of subjective freedom existing for-itself.

In the Remarks to § 301, Hegel makes it quite clear that the consultation of the Estates is a pure formality on the part of the bureaucracy, since actually the bureaucracy knows what is best for the people better than the people themselves; and in fact can operate quite well without the assistance of the Estates.

§ 301, *Remarks* (*cont*.) "The Estates start from isolated individuals, from a private point of view, from particular interests, and so are inclined to devote their activities to these at the expense of the general interests...."

All this is simply used by Hegel to argue his point that the Estates, with regard to their content, are a pure superfluity. They are the pure form of public will without content. And any form without content must be formless, i.e. the mere *appearance* of a form. Why then, does Hegel bring in the Estates at all? For the sake of logical completeness. He looks around for *being-for-itself*, and the Estates become the logical candidate. However, it would have been much more logical to start with the Estates as the implicit universal (the universal in-itself) and locate the explicit universal (the universal for-itself) in the executive. But for Hegel the actual is the rational, even if the actual is basically irrational. And the actuality here is the custom in modern states of contrasting the bureacracy as "public interest" with the Estates as "private interest." This is a metaphysical illusion, and it is quite in keeping with Hegel's viewpoint that he expresses this metaphysical illusion through the most illusory and "metaphysical" of all the powers of the State – the Estates.

§ 301, *Remarks* (*cont*.) "The specific function which the Concept assigns to the Estates is to be sought in the fact that in them the subjective moment in universal freedom ... comes into existence integrally related to the state."

Hegel's point is that just as the state enters into the people's subjective consciousness through the bureaucrats, the people (i.e. the subjective consciousness of civil society) begin to participate in the state through their delegates in the Estates. This is true. But it is a mistake to pass off this "beginning" of participation in an alien reality as the full reality.

§ 302. "The function [of the Estates] requires them to possess a political and administrative sense and temper, no less than a sense for the interests of individuals and particular groups.... They are a middle term preventing both the extreme isolation of the power of the crown ... and also the isolation of particular interests."

The general opposition between the nation and the executive power becomes epitomized in the Estates. This is why the Estates become the "middle term." In their mediating function, they take on the aspect of a miniature state to the people, and preserve the state from the threat of the disorganized masses precisely by disarming and disorganizing these masses. Insofar as they take on the appearance of the state, the state loses the appearance of an arbitrary tyranny. Insofar as they take on the appearance of a unified state within a state, the state loses the appearance of being a duality.

§ 302. *Remark* "It is one of the most important discoveries of logic that a specific moment, which, by standing in opposition, has the position of an extreme, ceases to be such and is a moment in an organic whole by being at the same time a mean."

The Estates in one sense represent substantial opposition to the Executive. But through their mediating function, they cease to be an "extreme," since they come to expend their energy on trifling and unsubstantial kinds of "opposition."

§ 303. "The universal class, or, more precisely, the class of civil servants, must, purely in virtue of its character as universal, have the universal as the end of its essential activity. In the Estates, as an element in the legislative power, the unofficial class acquires its political significance and efficacy."

To put it more plainly, in the Estates [the German word for Estates is *Stande*, Classes], the classes of civil society – i.e. the agricultural and business classes – are officially (politically) present as unofficial (unpolitical). Their relationship to the universal is simply a relationship of reflection, not a real relationship.

Hegel seems to forget that, according to his own premises, the identity of civil society and the state which existed in the middle ages became a separation. He seems to want to reestablish an identity where there is none.

§ 304. "The position of the [agricultural and business] classes is abstract to begin with, i.e. in contrast with the whole principle of monarchy or the crown their position is that of an extreme – empirical universality.... From the point of view of the classes, one moment in them must be adapted to the task of existing as in essence the moment of mediation."

The individuals in civil society exist as matter (the empirical universal) abstract from form. The member of civil society who participates in the Estates reproduces this abstraction in his own scism of roles: insofar as he enters into the "moment of mediation" he must cease to be a member of civil society, he must leave behind part of his essence: ["The separation of civil society and the political state appears necessarily to be a separation of the political citizen, the citizen of the state, from civil society, i.e., from his own actual, empirical reality." (p. 78)].

In the preceeding paragraphs (§§ 301–303) Hegel had spoken disparagingly of those who hold the "atomistic and abstract" view that the *individuals* of civil society should be represented directly in the legislature.* In a way, Hegel is right in observing that atomistic individuals cannot appear in the Estates, because the bureaucratic division which gives rise to the Estates *creates* an atomization of society which becomes incarnated as the essence of civil society. Civil society *qua* atomistic civil society must be forever outside the domain of the state: "The atomism into which civil society is driven ... results necessarily from the fact that the commonwealth [*das Gemeinwesen*], the communal being [*das kommunistische wesen*], within which the individual exists, is civil society separated from the state, or in other words, that the political state is an abstraction of civil society" (p. 79).

§ 303, *Remark* "The circles of association in civil society [Hegel continues] are already communities. To picture these communities as once more breaking up into a mere conglomeration of individuals as soon as they enter the field of politics ... is *eo ipso* to hold civil and political life apart from one another."

As a matter of fact, civil and political life *are* held apart from each other, and the communities of civil society *do* break up into conglomerations.

Just as Christians are equal in heaven but unequal on earth, modern man is equal in the political world but unequal in the social world. Why? Because modern man, especially since the French Revolution, has been separated from his universal social nature (which has been objectified in the formal organization of the *bureaucracy*), and has been left with nothing but the atomization of social life which is found in the classes of civil society. This atomization is not the result of the "sys-

* This view favors a "representative constitution," as opposed to the "Estate constitution" which Hegel favors. (See Marx, p. 76).

tem of needs," as Hegel thinks. But rather, it is the result of money and education – the final arbiters of the destiny of the "burgher."* The subjection of the members of civil society to such arbitrariness is then necessarily reflected in the "circles of association" in civil society, through which class differences become expressed (rather than transcended).

§ 304. "The estates, as an element in political life, still retain in their own significance the class distinctions already present in the lower spheres of civil life."

Here Hegel in his mystifying way tries to recapture the distinctions of civil society through a reflective *Reminiszenz* (reminiscence). According to the canons of his dialectic, these class distinctions should be transcended and yet preserved in the "reminiscence" of a higher form, as we proceed from civil society to political life. But in reality there is no *preservation* in this dialectical leap. If the classes of civil society attain any significance in the Estates, they do so only by sacrificing the significance they had in the non-political realm. There is no way they can preserve that significance, because they are functioning in an essentially dualistic society. Thus while Hegel tries to make it seem that the burgher as subject has two predicates – one of which represents simply a higher degree of the other – in reality he has created two subjects – the member of civil society and the member of the Estates – which cannot be made "identical" by any dialectical synthesis.

"The position of the classes . . . is abstract to begin with, i.e. in contrast with the whole principle of monarchy or the crown.... This abstract position changes into a rational relation ... only if the middle term between the opposites comes into existence.... From the point of view of the crown, the executive already has this character."

In other words, just as the crown would be the extreme of empirical singularity if it did not delegate some power to the executive, so also civil society would be the extreme of empirical universality if it did not find representation in and through the Estates. Thus the Estates are an extreme which has managed to transform itself into a middle term. Thus Hegel manages to mediate the opposition between the Crown and the nation through the use of two "middle terms" – the executive and the Estates. But he does not manage to explain away the *mutual* opposition that *still* remains between these two middle terms. And, in general, he is not referring to dialectic extremes here – extremes that call for mutual reconciliation – like North and South pole, masculinity and feminity, spiritualism and materialism. He is referring to extremes considered as independent entities – especially the "extreme of" the monarchy, which is self-sufficient and does not really need (in Hegel's philosophy) to be mediated with anything else. All this leads to a hodge-podge of pseudo-mediations: "The sovereign had to be the middle term in the legislature between the executive and the estates; but of course, the executive is the middle term between him and the Estates, and the Estates between him and civil society (p. 88)." These are all pseudo-mediations because the extremes are actual (i.e. non-dialectical): "Actual extremes cannot be mediated with each other precisely because they are actual extremes... The one does not carry in its womb the yearning, the need, the anticipation of the other (p. 89)." Thus, just as human and non-human cannot be mediated in the same way that male and female can be mediated, so also civil so-

* For this reason those who are without property and are dependent on their own labor are not, strictly speaking, part of civil society; but form a foundation upon which civil society is constructed (p. 81).

ciety and the state, etc. – cannot be mediated the way that they were mediated in the middle ages (when they existed in a state of identity). "The Estates are supposed to be the mediation between the crown and the executive on the one hand, and the crown and the people on the other. But they are not this, but rather the organized opposition to civil society.... Just as the sovereign democratizes himself in the executive, so this estate element must monarchize itself in its deputation (p. 93)."

§ 305. "The principle of one of the classes of civil society is in itself capable of adaptation to this political position."

This is the class of the landed gentry (the "agricultural class"), who receive representation in the Estates by tradition and by inheritance. According to Hegel, this class is one "whose basis is family life, and, so far as its livelihood is concerned, the possession of land."

It is noteworthy that Hegel tries to establish this class as the mediating element between the two major antitheses in the state – the Crown and civil society. This mediating "synthesis," however, is rather an anomaly because 1) the conflict between the two classes of civil society – the agricultural class and the business class – already destroys the possibility of any significant antithetical opposition breaking out between civil society and the Crown; 2) the synthesis is based on a non-political distinction (a distinction of civil society) and does not properly apply to the "political element" (the Estates in modern society)*; and 3) the fact that the agricultural class has its "basis in family life" is not too significant, since the same thing could be said about the business class.

"Its particular members attain their position by birth, just as the monarch does, and in common with him, they possess a will which rests on itself alone."

How does Hegel come to the conclusion that the will of this class "rests on itself alone"? [Marx objects,] "one should rather say a will which 'rests on ground and soil.' One should rather speak of a will resting on the disposition of the state...." (p. 95).

§ 306. [Hegel states that the wealth of the agricultural class becomes inalienable because of restrictions caused by the law of primogeniture. Marx goes on to comment on the "Addition" to this paragraph:]

§ 306, Addition "Primogeniture is grounded on the fact that the state should be able to reckon not on the bare possibility of political inclinations, but on something necessary. Now an inclination for politics is of course not bound up with wealth, but there is a relatively necessary connexion between the two, because a man with independent means is not hemmed in by external circumstances and so there is nothing to prevent him from entering politics and working for the state."

Hegel's argument here is that, even though the *possibility* of political inclinations is not sufficient for participation in government, the possession of "independent means" is sufficient grounds for assuring members of the agricultural class representation in the Estates, because wealth provides the *possibility* for fulfilling one's political inclinations. This argument is, to say the least, inconsistent; but there are

* "After he has developed the political Estates as a specific element, as a transubstantiation of the unofficial class into state citizenship... by what right does Hegel dissolve this organism once more into the distinction of the unofficial class, and thus into the unofficial class, and then derive from it the political state's mediation with itself?" (p. 95).

also other grounds on which we can take exception to the importance of primogeniture in peopling the Estates with politicians:

The law of primogeniture seems to be in contradiction to principles that Hegel himself has already defended in the *Philosophy of Right*: for example, the principle that property is a predicate of the subjective will (§. 65), and the principle that one's freedom of will is inalienable (§. 66). Since primogeniture makes the free disposition of property subservient to the accidents of birth, and makes the family subservient to (the predicate of) property laws – the proper Hegelian order seems to be inverted.* Also, Hegel contradicts his principle (§. 158) that the basis for family life is love (a love which should extend to all the children, and not just the first born); and his principle that in the sphere of contracts "I hold property not merely by means of a thing and my subjective will, but by means of another person's will as well" (p. 71) – a situation that does not seem to obtain in the case of primogeniture. Likewise, he seems to contradict his definition of the political sentiment as the "trust that my interest, both substantive and particular, is contained and preserved in ... the state's interest" (p. 268); since in the Addition to p. 306 Hegel indicates quite clearly that the political disposition is, in the case of the landed gentry, independent of the state and based purely on property qualifications. Finally, we might note that Hegel also seems to weaken his former statement about the "independence" of *civil servants* (who, unlike the landed gentry, are dependent on the state treasury for their salary); and he even puts philosophy in a bad light since, as he states in the Preface, philosophy in modern Germany is a profession which is dependent on the government treasury.

All in all, the thrust of Hegel's approval of primogeniture as a means for determining representatives of the Estates, is to erect raw, unconscious matter (the land, which has not even been sublimated to private property in a social and human sense) into an independent power capable of superceding all the volitional elements in the state constitution, and remaining as the "incorruptible" basis for the establishment of a certain element in political life.

§ 307. "The right of this section of the agricultural class is thus based in a way on the natural principle of the family. But this principle is at the same time reversed owing to hard sacrifices made for political ends, and thereby the activity of this class is essentially directed to those ends. As a consequence of this, this class is summoned and entitled to its political vocation by birth without the hazards of election."

We have already seen how the "natural principle of the family" is reversed by the institution of primogeniture. It reverses the principle of love, which is the basis of family life. But according to Hegel the only reversal brought about by primogeniture is the reversal of the private status of the family. According to him, the families of the landed gentry become oriented by vocation to public (political) service, and thus go beyond the call of duty that would apply to the ordinary family. Thus he tries to justify the emergence of entailed estates to political stature, on the basis of an accident of birth.

Here Hegel's idealism seems to catch up with him. Having disdained nature so often, he is now driven to assert the preeminence of nature (i.e. the accident of

* "Private property (landed property) is fortified against the owner's own wilfulness by having the sphere of his wilfulness suddenly changed from a universal human sphere to the specific wilfulness of private property. In other words, private property has become the subject of the will, and the will is merely the predicate of private property" (p. 101).

birth, giving rise to this physical body, endowed *ipso facto* with these political traits) over the human will (i.e. over the right of the human will to aspire to political service or to choose between those who thus aspire). At any rate, Hegel helps us understand why it is that the aristocracy takes such pride in blood and ancestry. For the secret of the power of the aristocracy is to be found in zoology! And heraldry as a science is cognate with zoology.

Just as Hegel erects abstract personality (the indeterminate "capricious" will) into the highest political personality (the monarch), so also here he erects abstract private property into the highest right of the state. In effect, the laws regarding private property become the *sine qua non*, the foundation of the constitution. All human endeavors and choices become subservient to this foundation. And since the foundation of the constitution is, in a certain sense, the constitution itself – we might say that the constitutional monarchy in a state like modern Germany is the constitution *of* private property.

Thus the Germans have surpassed the Romans in their allegiance to private property. In Rome, when the development of private property had reached its zenith, primogeniture allowed for willfullness on the part of the testator. What is more, state-honors were never hereditary, and a distinction was always made between private property as a *factum*, an existing fact, and private property as a right (grounded in various legal determinations). But in Germany the rationalism of the Romans has been developed into a mysticism where blood and property and political power are tied up into an ineffable unity.

§ *308.* "The second section of the Estates comprises the fluctuating element in civil society. This element can enter politics only through its deputies; the multiplicity of its members is an external reason for this, but the essential reason is the specific character of this element and its activity.... Society makes the appointment [of the deputies] *as* a society, articulated into associations, communities, and corporations...."

The "fluctuating element" in civil society, i.e. the business class, is presented as relatively unstable by Hegel, even though he endows it with quite a lot of stability in giving it access to the political sphere through the corporations, associations, etc. – whose permanence and stability is assured under the present scheme of things. The members of the business class do not automatically become members of the Chamber of Deputies (unlike the members of the landed gentry, who are automatically assured of membership in the Chamber of Peers). Hegel says that the "multiplicity of its members" is only the external reason for this. He wants to offer a reason which is essential, not quantitative. And the essential reason which he comes up with is that the organic nature of the State-idea requires that members of civil society should be able to enter the "political" sphere only through its larger, more generic articulations – the corporations, etc. Thus he is concerned with the essential aspects, rather than the existential aspects. But in reality the existential and quantitative aspects are the most important in this question, and should not have been ignored by Hegel (p. 117). (In other words, if it were not for the vast number of members of the business classes, there is no reason why they should not be assured of *direct* participation in the Estates.)

§ *308, Remarks* "To hold that every single person should share in deliberating and deciding on political matters of general concern on the ground that all individuals are members of the state, that its concerns are their concerns ... is tantamount to a proposal to put the democratic element without any rational form into the organism of the state...."

Hegel's treatment of this question has to be understood against the background of the utter separation of civil society from the political (i.e. the social) existence of society. In "civil society," as Hegel presents it, man lives an abstract non-political and a-social existence. He is dissolved into atomic individuality, and is saved from complete isolation only because of his instinctive tendency to join corporations, etc., which connect him "organically" to the processes which bring about the "representation" of civil society in the Chamber of Deputies. The answer that Hegel gives to the problem of representation is dictated by his formulation of the ideal of constitutional monarchy: "The question of whether all as individuals are members of the legislature or whether they should enter the legislature through deputies is the placing in question of the representative principle within the representative principle, i.e. within that fundamental conception of the political state which exists in constitutional monarchy" (p. 119). Hegel does not envision a situation where each member of the "empirical universality" should become a full participant in the concerns of the "actually existing universal." In order to achieve this latter end, he would have to establish the right of suffrage for civil society – a right which would lead towards the abrogation of the present political order: "The vote is the chief political interest of civil society. In unrestricted suffrage, both active and passive, civil society has actually raised itself for the first time to an abstraction of itself, to political existence as its true universal and essential existence. But the full achievement of this abstraction is at once also the transcendence of the abstraction" (p. 121).

§ 309. "Since deputies are elected to deliberate and decide on *public* affairs, the point about their election is that it is a choice of individuals on the strength of confidence felt in them, i.e., a choice of such individuals as have a better understanding of these affairs . . . and such also as essentially vindicate the universal interest. . . ."

This makes little sense because, if the deputies are really to concern themselves with public interests as opposed to private, they cannot conscientiously act as delegates of the corporations, etc. (i.e. the private interests).

If the electors of the deputies had any political power themselves, and were simply choosing to delegate that power to their deputies – this representation here would be meaningful. But they have no such choice. And in the context of the system under which they are operating, to choose a delegate means to separate that delegate from any answerability to his electors – so that he is not, in any real sense, *their* "deputy."

§ 309, (*Addition*) "Representation is grounded on trust. . . ."
§ 310. "The guarantee that deputies will have the qualifications and disposition that accord with this end [managing the affairs of their electors] . . . is to be found . . . above all in the knowledge of the organization and interests of the state and civil society, the temperament, and the skill which a deputy acquires . . . and then evinces in his action."

Formerly Hegel proposed the Chamber of Peers as a guarantee against the [untrustworthy] dispositions of the chamber of Deputies; and now he proposes tests to guarantee that the Deputies will have trustworthy dispositions.

Hegel has also just said (§ 309, Addition) that the trust and confidence of the elector was the guarantee of the deputy; but now we further require some guarantee of the deputy's *ability*.

And what kind of ability does he look for? Bureaucratic ability – the disposition which will be acceptable to the executive (although he had formerly proposed the executive as a power in opposition to the Deputies).

§ *310, Remark* "[The state] can recognize in individuals only their objectively recognizable and tested character, and it must be all the more careful ... since this section[the Deputies] is rooted in interests and activities directed towards the particular...."

In other words, the state would like the deputies to be reduplications of the executive bureaucrats.

§ *311.* "A further point about the election of deputies is that, since civil society is the electorate, the deputies should themselves be conversant with and participate in its special needs, difficulties, and particular interests. Owing to the nature of civil society, its deputies are the deputies of the various Corporations.... Hence the deputies *eo ipso* adopt the point of view of society, and their actual election is therefore either something wholly superfluous or else reduced to a trivial play of opinion and caprice."

The first sentence of this paragraph contradicts § 309, which asserts that the deputies should essentially vindicate the universal (not the particular) interest.

The second sentence contradicts the spirit of § 310, which states that the deputies should have a managerial and political sense (not a Corporation and civil sense).

The third sentence contradicts the Addition to § 309, which asserts that the election of the delegates is a fulfillment of trust (not something "superfluous" or "capricious").

[Marx then goes on to quote § 312 and § 313, in which Hegel claims that the Chamber of the Deputies, because of its special mediating function, must be completely separate from the other Chamber. Marx ends on a note of exasperation, exclaiming "Oh, Jesus!"]

2. Sovereignty in relation to foreign states

The internal nature of the state, which draws all the state's organic branches and elements into a negative unity,* manifests itself externally as a negative relationship to finite aspects of foreign states. This is the rational basis for *war* (an extreme type of external negation).

War, which (like all other relationships to foreign states) is primarily subject to the decisions of the sovereign, is necessary in order that infinite Spirit may demonstrate that the finite is *really* finite. What the preachers tell us about so often from the pulpits – that finite things are transient and should not be objects of attachment – becomes a *de facto* reality in and through war. In the course of a war, a nation disengages itself from its accidental embodiments, and thus indirectly secures for itself a higher substantial unity, and greater internal unity and peace.

A standing army, which is necessary for counteracting threats to this or that particular aspect of a state's existence, is a particular class embodying a particular virtue – *courage*. The virtue of military courage is noteworthy, insofar as it is the manifestation of all the paradoxes of existence in highly developed ethical communities – e.g., the fact that one finds his freedom only in self-sacrifice, that one finds his individuality only as a cog in the spiritual machinery of the state, that one attains the highest presence of spirit only in in the renunciation of his own spirit (i.e., through the absolute, unquestioning obedience of the soldier), and so forth. (These motives do not, however, have to be explicit to the mind of the soldier; only a general sentiment of patriotism.)

In the event that not just *particular* aspects of the state, but the existence of the state as a whole – is threatened – then *total mobilization* of the citizenry is called for; and ordinary citizens must display the same spirit of sacrifice and sense of duty as animates the professional army.

*Kant's notion of "Perpetual Peace"*** would be an impossibility. Even if various nations band together as a group (cf. The Holy Alliance), they will naturally become oriented to other *groups* as enemies (i.e., as objects of finite, extrinsic *negation*). And besides, "perpetual peace" would be a disaster to the existence of sovereign states. For nothing assures the atrophy and corruption of the various organizations and structures of a state more than prolonged periods of peace. War with other countries generates that spirit of national unity which is indispensable for the health and stability of

---

* The state is a "negative" unity in much the same sense that the hand and its fingers are a negative unity: the hand must negate (be distinct from) the fingers in order to be effectively joined *with* the fingers, and to form a unity-in-distinction.

** Immanuel Kant wrote a treatise entitled, "Perpetual Peace."

the state as an *organism which transcends and holds together its individual components.*

B. *International law*

When an individual state advances to the point where it has superceded the conflicts of abstract universal right versus abstract particular welfare (in other words, when it becomes a *concrete, individual** state) it becomes related to other states as one *concrete individual* related to another. The relation *among* individual states is one in which each is seeking primarily its own welfare, in an autonomous way.

If and when a state has an autonomous *content*, it is natural that this content should take on the *form* of autonomy, by means of formal recognition from other states. This would imply that each state, while not remaining indifferent to the domestic welfare of other states, would recognize the essential autonomy of those other states as far as regards the conduct of their own domestic affairs.

However, it is inevitable that the interests of states will often conflict with other states (just as the interests of members of civil society often conflict) – and this leads to the formation of interim contracts, i.e., treaties. "*International law*" in the context of such treaties, merely implies that such treaties "ought" to be kept. However, this "ought" must remain a perpetual "ought,' since the sovereignty of a nation gives it the right to break off relations with other nations at any time. The act of breaking off diplomatic relations automatically dissolves contractual obligations, because of the absence of any supervening international juridical power.

Even if nations should create such an international judicial power through a "league of nations," that power could never have absolute jurisdictional authority, since the authority of each state is already absolute. For a sovereign state is not like an abstract** person, who becomes related to other abstract persons according to universal abstract "moral" laws. A state is a concrete type of existence, and thus supersedes the sphere of abstract morality altogether. Thus "ought" for a state means something different than "ought" for a free individual.

However, there is an incentive for peace in the very fact that war is essentially a manifestation of the *transitory* nature of finitude – and therefore is something that ought to pass away. Thus the *jus gentium*, which is ordained to assure that wars will be transitory, and that wars in progress will not directly affect the ability of noncombatants to recover, etc., – is valid.

* See The Glossary for the special Hegelian meanings of "concrete" and "individual."
** See Glossary for the Hegelian meaning of "abstract."

The courtesy and civility of nations, whether at war or at peace, with one another, has its immediate basis in the inner universality of custom – a similarity of mores among certain nations which leads them to naturally respect each other's envoys and prisoners; or (during peace time) to grant rights of trade, travel, and communication to foreign subjects.

– Transition to world history

The dialectical interplay of finite national spirits among each other leads to, and is superseded by, the infinity of universal spirit which is to be found in *world history*.

C. World history

The Idea of the unity-in-distinction of subjective and objective exists in *art* as intuitition and depiction; in *religion* as feeling and imagination; in *philosophy* as thought; and finally, in World History as a concrete actuality in which all abstract elements are dissolved and transformed.

The various national spirits, each in their turn, emerge from immediacy (nomadic, pastoral, agricultural states; or patriarchal forms of governments) to self-consciousness. They are impelled by necessity to freedom, and to self-knowledge (and thus also to spiritual betterment). These various national spirits are diversified in space (geographically) and in time, in accord with their finite nature. Those which, at any time, best approximate to the ideal notion of a state, and, moreover, best promote the designs of world history (the universal judging the particular) – are the harbingers of the world spirit, and *must* be successful and victorious. Such nations reach their zenith, and then decline. They may sometimes prevent their absolute disintegration by adapting to the new designs of the world spirit which appear on the horizon; but they will adapt to it as to an adopted child – not as to something arising out of them spontaneously.

The progress of the world spirit to self-knowledge reveals itself in four stages:

a) *The Oriental world*, the immediate stage of existence in which everything – religion, philosophy, politics, art – is interfused; and in which no real distinctions are allowed to emerge. Only static, ossified distinctions, such as "castes," are tolerated.

b) *The Greek world*, the stage of the aesthetic union of immediacy and self-consciousness, developed and distributed among various city-states by a central authority. (A class of slaves, however, was necessary to make this kind of existence possible).

c) *The Roman World*, which ,before the time of Christ, manifested the conflict between universality and abstract self-consciousness (in the rivalry between the aristocracy and the plebs) – and then dissolved into ineffectiveness after the advent of Christianity.

d) *The Germanic World*, which manifested the reconciliation of the divine and human, of universality and particularity, first of all in a primitive way (in barbarian eras) and finally in the modern constitutional monarchy.*

SAMPLE EXAMINATION QUESTIONS

1. One of the distinctive features of Hegel's political philosophy is that he views the state as an organism rather than as an organization. Explain the meaning of this distinction. What would be some of the implications of viewing the state as an organism?
2. How does Hegel characterize the ideal relationship between Church and State?
3. On what basis does Hegel object to the traditional notion of the "3 types of government" (monarchy, aristocracy, and democracy)? What does he offer as a substitute for this traditional notion?
4. What are the three main branches of the state, according to Hegel? How does his tri-partite division compare to our tri-partite "balance of power" system?
5. How does Hegel defend sovereignty-by-birth? What unfavorable consequences does he predict for governments which have no "ruling family"?
6. What is the Hegelian ideal of a "public executive"? What steps does Hegel suggest should be taken to assure that such executives be chosen exclusively on the basis of their talents and skills?
7. What is Hegel's opinion concerning "public opinion" and censorship?
8. Hegel argues that it is impossible for one nation to make a stable and perpetually binding treaty with another nation. What reasons does he give for this contention?

TERM PAPER TOPICS

1. *The influence of Hegel's "Philosophy of Right" upon Marx.* It can be shown that Marx arrived at his earliest ideas on property, the proletariat, and communism in his critique of Hegel's *Philosophy of Right*. See Shlomo Avineri's article, "The Hegelian Origins of Marx's Political Thought," in *The Review of Metaphysics*, Sept. 1967; also, "Perspectives in the Marxian Critique of Hegel's Political Philosophy," in Pelczynski's *Hegel's Political Philosophy*.* For a longer discussion of this topic, see the early chapters of Avineri's *Social and Political Thought of Karl Marx*.**

---

* Such as existed in Prussia in Hegel's time, as well as other countries. It should be noted that "Germanic" comprises many European countries besides "Germany proper." England in this sense is "Germanic."
** See Bibliography.

2. *Hegel's theory on war.* It is not strange that Hegel's statements about the "necessity" of war should elicit a strong interest, especially in these post-atom-bomb years. A number of articles have been written on this topic: Smith, "Hegel on War" (Journal of the History of Ideas, 1965, pp. 282–5); Avineri, "The Problem of War in Hegel's Thought" (Journal of the History of Ideas, 1961, pp. 463–74); Bruggen-cate, "Hegel's Views of War," *The Philosophical Quarterly,* 1950, pp. 58–60, and Verene, "Hegel's Account of War" in *Hegel's Political Philosophy* (Pelczynski ed.).* Also, see Immanuel Kant's *Perpetual Peace* (Liberal Arts Library) – a short treatise in which Kant proposes means for attaining the ideal of universal peace among nations. Hegel's "bellicose" statements towards the end of the *Philosophy of Right* are fundamentally a reaction to Kant's proposals in this treatise.

3. *The relationship of punishment to crime, according to Hegel.* For a fuller discussion of this topic, see Flechteim, "Hegel and the Problem of Punishment" (*Journal of the History of Ideas,* 1947, pp. 293–308); also Doyle, "Justice and Legal Punishment" (*Philosophy,* Jan. 1967, pp. 53–670; and Cooper, "Hegel's Theory of Punishment," in *Hegel's Political Philosophy* (Pelczynski ed.)*.

4. *The sources of Hegel's political thought.* For an extensive discussion of Hegel's indebtedness to Rousseau, Kant and Fichte, see *Idealism, Politics and History,* by George Kelly.* Kelly also includes, at the end of this book, an exhaustive bibliography of books and articles dealing with Hegelian and pre-Hegelian political thought.

5. *Hegel and Naziism.* Peter Viereck, in *Metapolitics* (Capricorn) shows how the doctrines of National Socialism in Germany of the 1920's were based on the Hegelian notion of the state as an "organism," and also on a peculiar interpretation of Hegel's statement (*Philosophy of Right,* p. 10) that "the Rational is the Real (or Actual)." The Nazis took this statement to mean that a nation's policies are correct ("rational") when they are successful ("realistic," or "real"). However, all Hegel means by this statement is that the *primary reality* (or actuality) in the world as a a whole is the *rational* unity of opposites – of subject and object, of thought and being, of the "is" and the "ought," of society and the individual. See my notes on Hegel's Preface, p. 13; on the "Absolute Will," p. 15; and on the State, p. 44; also Avineri, *Hegel's Theory of the Modern State* (see Biblio.), p. 118–130.

6. Hegel has often been accused of political conservatism, i.e. supporting the rather repressive Prussian regime under which he lived in his later years, and opposing major movements of political reform during his time. Shlomo Avineri, in *Hegel's Theory of the Modern State* (see Biblio.) tries to show that Hegel's apparent conservatism was primarily directed at conserving the *reforms* that had taken place in Germany under influence of the French Revolution (see pp. 69ff, 79, 123–130, 182). He also points out that some of the major policies advocated in the *Philosophy of Right* went against the established practices of the Prussian government (see pp. 115–116, 191,192)

Kaufmann's *Hegel's Political Philosophy* (see Biblio.) is a series of debates in which Sydney Hook and E. F. Carritt, critics of Hegel's political philosophy, lock horns with Hegel's defenders – T. M. Knox, S. Avineri and Z. A. Pelczynski – on such topics as Hegel's reputed conservatism, Prussianism and nationalism.

SAMPLE ESSAYS

1. In the beginning of Hegel's discussion of the State, he shows how there is a natural reciprocity of rights and duties in a fully developed state. There can be no rights without duties, no duties without rights. He concludes (in § 261) that slavery is irrational because of this. The slave really has *no* duties, no ethical responsibilities, because he has been denied basic human rights. Likewise, if we were to ask, "why has the slave no *rights*?" the answer would be that he is not considered to be a responsible contributor to society, *freely* fulfilling his *duties* for the common good. Rather, he does what he does out of compulsion, without any sense of duty; he has no "position of responsibility,' in the usual sense of that phrase. Discuss the wider implications of the "reciprocity of rights and duties," not only as regards slavery, but also as regards the situation of socially oppressed individuals or groups.

2. (a) Without a constitutional, hereditary monarch, according to Hegel, there can be no ultimate, absolute decision-making power in the state. A nation which lacks such a monarch is doomed to lengthy delays at times of crisis, when quick decisions are called for; is doomed to making vacillating decisions, which can always be overturned by an act of the legislature or a judicial decision. Since Hegel's time, most constitutional monarchies in *Hegel's* sense of that word (England would not seem to completely qualify) have disappeared from the world. Has Hegel's analysis proved to be true? Aside from dictatorships (which do not meet Hegel's criterion of a free state), do modern republics give indication of being more vacillating, less stable and consistent, than the former constitutional monarchies? If so, are they any critical dangers germane to the "unwieldy" characteristics of modern republics or democracies? Would they still be preferable, because of certain strong points that Hegel was not aware of? Are there any potentially fatal weaknesses in *Hegel's* ideal of a free monarchical form of government?

(b) In spite of Hegel's apparent advocacy of a strong monarchy, Avineri in *Hegel's Theory of the Modern State*, pp. 187–188 (see Biblio.) maintains that the "sovereignty" of the monarch in Hegel's estimation, was largely symbolic. The question of whether Hegel believed in a symbolic or a really effective monarchy might perhaps be resolved by making a distinction between sovereignty as a domestic attribute and as a factor in relating to foreign nations. This latter distinction is analyzed in Pelczynski, *Hegel's Political Philosophy* (see Biblio.), pp. 230–232. However, it should be noted that in § 279 (Addition), Hegel states that the monarchy in England (which had and has a largely symbolic function), was lacking in (domestic) sovereignty. Does this indicate that Hegel favored a monarchy with more than a symbolic function? Students of history or political science may be interested in discussing Hegel's observations in § 279, with reference to the factual political circumstances at the time the *Philosophy of Right* was published (1821).

APPENDIX*

MARX'S COMMENTARY (pp. 131–142)

A Contribution to the Critique . . . An Introduction

The critique of religion is the prerequisite for all critique, since religion supplies the background for all the "secular" illusions of modern man. Once man is freed from the illusions of happiness, he will be ready to attain to real happiness. (By "man" here, we mean "the world of man, the state, society." p. 131).

We are concerned in particular here with the German philosophy of the state – which is patterned after the prototype of a religious illusion.

The Germans, unlike the *ancien régimes*, are not sincere in their adherence to the *status quo*. The demise of the *ancien régimes* was tragic, but that of the German political system will be comic, since it was never consciously accepted in the first place. In fact, Germany lives in the future – through its philosophy – although its political *status quo* is an anachronism. And one who would try to alter this political system must do so through a critique of – a hand-to-hand combat with – its philosophical reflection (which has caught up with what in other countries have been practical developments). The "practical" political party in Germany which would like to bypass philosophy, tries to transcend philosophy without actualizing it – which is impossible in Germany. The "theoretical" party, on the other hand, tries to actualize philosophy without transcending it – [which is simply to perpetuate an inverted and alienated world.]

What is the answer for Germany? Philosophical criticism, joined with material force (the "criticism of weapons"). The role of philosophical criticism (theory) is to become transformed into material force, once it has seized the masses, and become *praxis*. Then something on the analogy of the Protestant Reformation will take place: "If the Protestant transformation of the German laity into priests emancipated the lay popes . . . so the philosophical transformation of the priestly Germans into men will emancipate the people." (p. 138).

But what class will supply the material basis for the revolution in Germany? Here Germany's situation differs from a nation like France, in which the torch of political awareness passes now to one class and now to another. In Germany,

---

* Marx intended to write a "revised version" of the commentary which has been paraphrased in this handbook. He eventually gave up this plan, but not before writing an Introduction to the proposed revision. This Introduction is included in the O'Malley-Jolin edition, pp. 131 ff. as an "Appendix." A summary of the Introduction, which contains some seminal ideas about the proletariat, is included here.

there is no real political awareness except in the form of political philosphy (as befits a theoretical people).* And Germany is so undeveloped in the practical sphere that there can be no world-historical significance given to this or that particular class. Therefore the class which will spearhead the German revolution will not be any particular class, but the dissolution of all classes, the object of universal wrong – the "dissolution of society existing as a particular class." (p. 142). This is the proletariat, which embodies the negation of private property. This class is just beginning to form in Germany, as a result of industrial development and the dissolution of the middle class. The imperious need of this class is what will overcome the incessant dichotomy between theory and praxis, between intellectual and practical life, in modern Germany.

* "Is there any country in the world which shares as naively as so-called constitutional Germany all the illusions of the constitutional regime without any of its realities?" (p. 139).

SUGGESTED READING ON HEGEL AND/OR MARX'S INTERPRETATION OF HEGEL

Avineri, Shlomo, *Hegel's Theory of the Modern State* (Cambridge: University Press, 1972)

Avineri, Shlomo, *The Social and Political Thought of Karl Marx* (Cambridge: University Press, 1968)

Cairns, Huntington, *Legal Philosophy from Plato to Hegel* (Baltimore: Johns Hopkins Press, 1949)

Dupré, Louis, *The Philosophical Foundations of Marxism* (New York: Harcourt, Brace and World, 1966)

Foster, Michael, *The Political Philosophies of Plato and Hegel* (Oxford: Clarendon Press, 1935)

Gray, J. Glenn, *Hegel and Greek Thought* (New York: Harper, 1968)

Hegel, G. W. F., *Philosophy of Right*, Knox tr. (Oxford: 1967)

Kaufmann, W., *Hegel's Political Philosophy* (N.Y.P. Atherton Press, 1970)

Kelly, George, *Idealism, Politics and History: Sources of Hegelian Thought* (Cambridge: University Press, 1969)

Löwith, Karl, *From Hegel to Nietzsche* (New York: Anchor, 1964)

Marcuse, Herbert, *Reason and Revolution: Hegel and the Rise of Social Theory* (New York: Beacon, 1968)

Marx, Karl, *Critique of Hegel's Philosophy of Right*, Tr. by Joseph O'Malley and Anita Jolin (Cambridge: University Press, 1971)

Mehta, Vrajendra raj. *Hegel and the Modern State: An Introduction to Hegel's Political Thought*, (New Delhi: Associated Publishing House, 1968)

Pelcynski, A. A., *Hegel's Political Philosophy* (Cambridge: The University Press, 1971)

Plant, Raymond, *Hegel* (Bloomington: Indiana University Press, 1973)

Stace, W. T., *The Philosophy of Hegel* (New York: Dover, 1955) (see the sections on "morality" and "objective spirit.")

Walsh, W. H. *Hegelian Ethics* (New York: St. Martin's Press, 1969)

INDEX OF NAMES

Aristotle, 1, 2
Bosanquet, B., 4
Descartes, 1,
Fichte, 2, 13, 50, 80
Husserl, 3
Kant, 1, 2, 3, 24, 50, 80
Kierkegaard, 2, 3
Marx & Marxism, 2, 3, 4, 11, 12
Mill, J. S., 24

Montesquieu, 50
Napoleon, 50
Plato, 13, 32
Rousseau, 44, 80
Schelling, 2
Smith, Adam, 33
Spinoza, 2
Viereck, P., 4
von Heller, 50

SUBJECT INDEX

the "Absolute", 10
"abstract", 10
the agricultural class, 35, 69, 70 f.
alienation (in civil society), 68 f.
aristocracy, 50, 79
art, 46, 77 f.
the bourgeois ("burgher"), 32, 61 f., 69 f.
the bureaucracy, 35, 61 ff., 67 ff., 72
burgher (see Bourgeois)
the business class, 35, 69, 73
capital, 29, 34 f.
categories, 1
the Catholic Church, 62, 82
censorship, 65
children, 29
the Christian Religion, 32, 46, 54, 69, 77 f.
  82
the Church, (see Christian Religion)
civil servants (see Bureaucracy)
civil society, 26, 32 ff., 44, 47 f., 61 f., 64 f.,
  69 f., 73 f.
the clan, 29
classes, social, 34 f. (see also Agricultural
  Class, Business Class, and Bureaucracy)
colonization, 41
commodities, 34
the Concept, 11, 14
"concrete", 10
conscience, 23, 25
the "conservatism" of Hegel, 80
the Constitution, 45 ff., 54, 66 f., 73, 79
contract, 20, 28, 29, 72, 77
corporations, 33, 40ff., 46, 60, 65, 73
crime, 21, 38, 40f., 53, 58, 60
the Crown, 50ff., 64
custom, 78
democracy, 4, 5, 50, 56f., 66, 81
the Deputies, 65, 73ff.
dialectical logic, 6, 7
the "division of labor", 34

divorce, 28, 30
duty, 23, 45, 47, 81
education, 29, 32ff., 46, 70
emigration, 41
The Encyclopedia of Philosophy, by G. W.
  F. Hegel, 6
England, 37, 52, 58, 79n., 81
equality, political, 19, 36
equity, courts of, 39
the Estates, 64f., 67ff.
the executive branch of government, 50,
  60ff., 63, 70, 75
"existence in-self, -for-self, -in-and-for-
  self", 7, 8, 9
existentialism, 2
the family, 26, 27ff., 47f., 61, 71f.
femininity, 28, 31
foreign relation (see International Relations)
France, 44, 69, 80, 82
freedom, 25, 29, 56, 72, 76, 78
gentry, landed (see Agricultural Class)
God, 46, 79
the "Good", 23, 24
the Greek city-state, 26, 32, 56
history, World, 78ff.
The History of Philosophy, by G. W. F.
  Hegel, 2
human nature, 33
the Idea, 10, 11, 32, 34, 47f.
immediacy, 11, 78f.
incest, 29
individuality, 10, 76
inheritance, 30, 65 (see also Primogeniture)
international relations, 76ff.
the Judiciary, 33, 38f., 50, 77
the Jury, 39
justice, 36
law, 4, 8, 14, 35, 36ff.
the Legislative, 50, 64ff., 67f.

The Logic, by G. W. F. Hegel, 5, 48, 49
love, 27ff., 48, 72
luxury, 34
machines, 34
manufacturing, 35
marriage, 27ff., 35
masculinity, 28
Masonic rites, 63
mediation, 11, 70f.
the military, 67, 76
Mind (see "Spirit")
monarchy, 50, 54ff., 70f., 79, 81 (see also "the Crown")
Monasticism, 28
money, 29, 64, 70
morality, 4, 8, 14, 15, 21, 22ff., 35, 77
National Socialism, 4, 80
nationalism, 58, 80
Naziism (see National Socialism)
need, 32ff.
nomadic existence, 35
"objectivity", 1, 3
the "ought", 13, 21, 25, 36, 77
particularity, 9, 13, 20, 21, 32, 42, 55
patriotism, 76
peace, 55, 76ff., 80
Peers, Chamber of, 73ff.
personality, 15, 18, 19, 21, 28f., 32, 54ff., 58, 77
phenomenology, 2
The Phenomenology of Mind, by G. W. F. Hegel, 2, 3, 10
philosophy, 4, 8, 13, 14, 46, 72, 78, 82
The Philosophy of Nature, by G. W. F. Hegel, 5
The Philosophy of Spirit (*Mind*), 6
police, 33, 40
politics, participation in, 71, 73f.
polygamy, 28
poverty, 40f.
"predicaments", 1
primogeniture, 58, 65, 71f.
the proletariat, 4, 11, 62, 69

property, private, 4, 11, 15, 19, 20, 29, 36, 38, 56, 72, 73
Protestantism, 46, 82
punishment, 21, 39
Reason, 10, 13, 33
"refinement", 34
the republic, 56f., 81 (see also Democracy)
revolution, 64, 65, 66f., 74, 80f.
right, 4, 8, 14, 20, 36, 45, 47, 81
Rome, 32, 73
Russia, 63
"Science", 10
Scotland, 58
selling, 20
sex (see Masculinity, Femininity)
slavery, 30
"social contract", 44
sovereignty, 52, 55, 76f., 81
Spain, 50
"species-forms", 56
Spirit (or Mind), 10, 27
the State, 4, 11, 13, 15, 26, 32, 44ff., 66f., 68, 76f.
"subjectivity", 1, 3
suffrage, 74
taxes, 41, 64, 67
"thesis, antithesis, synthesis" (see "existence in-self, -for-self, -in-and-for-self")
the tribe, 29
treaties, 77
Understanding, 10, 33, 53
universality, 10, 13, 15, 20, 21, 32, 37, 42, 55
value, 34
violence (see Crime)
war, 54f., 76, 77f., 80
welfare, 23, 41
will, 8, 9, 14, 71f.
— determinate will, 8, 9, 15, 54
— indeterminate will, 8, 9, 15, 44, 54, 73
— absolute will, 8, 9, 15, 19, 22, 26
work, 33
wrong, 20, 21, 22